PHYSICS IN
OUR WORLD

ELECTRICITY and MAGNETISM

Kyle Kirkland, Ph.D.

Facts On File
An imprint of Infobase Publishing

ELECTRICITY AND MAGNETISM

Facts On File, Inc.
An imprint of Infobase Publishing
132 West 31st Street
New York NY 10001

ISBN-10: 0-8160-6112-2
ISBN-13: 978-0-8160-6112-9

Library of Congress Cataloging-in-Publication Data

Kirkland, Kyle.
    Electricity and magnetism / Kyle Kirkland.
        p. cm.—(Physics in our world)
    Includes bibliographical references and index.
    ISBN 0-8160-6112-2
1. Electricity. 2. Magnetism. I. Title. II. Series.
    QC522.K57 2007
    537—dc22   2006013783

Text design by Kerry Casey
Cover design by Dorothy M. Preston
Illustrations by Richard Garratt

Printed in the United States of America
MP FOF 10 9 8 7 6 5 4 3 2

This book is printed on acid-free paper.

❋ Contents ❋

❋ PREFACE ❋

THE NUCLEAR BOMBS that ended World War II in 1945 were a convincing and frightening demonstration of the power of physics. A product of some of the best scientific minds in the world, the nuclear explosions devastated the Japanese cities of Hiroshima and Nagasaki, forcing Japan into an unconditional surrender. But even though the atomic bomb was the most dramatic example, physics and physicists made their presence felt throughout World War II. From dam-breaking bombs that skipped along the water to submerged mines that exploded when they magnetically sensed the presence of a ship's hull, the war was as much a scientific struggle as anything else.

World War II convinced everyone, including skeptical military leaders, that physics is an essential science. Yet the reach of this subject extends far beyond military applications. The principles of physics affect every part of the world and touch on all aspects of people's lives. Hurricanes, lightning, automobile engines, eyeglasses, skyscrapers, footballs, and even the way people walk and run must follow the dictates of scientific laws.

The relevance of physics in everyday life has often been overshadowed by topics such as nuclear weapons or the latest theories of how the universe began. Physics in Our World is a set of volumes that aims to explore the whole spectrum of applications, describing how physics influences technology and society, as well as helping people understand the nature and behavior of the universe and all its many interacting parts. The set covers the major branches of physics and includes the following titles:

♦ *Force and Motion*

♦ *Electricity and Magnetism*

- *Time and Thermodynamics*
- *Light and Optics*
- *Atoms and Materials*
- *Particles and the Universe*

Each volume explains the basic concepts of the subject and then discusses a variety of applications in which these concepts apply. Although physics is a mathematical subject, the focus of these books is on the ideas rather than the mathematics. Only simple equations are included. The reader does not need any special knowledge of mathematics, although an understanding of elementary algebra would be helpful in a few cases. The number of possible topics for each volume is practically limitless, but there is only room for a sample; regrettably, interesting applications had to be omitted. But each volume in the set explores a wide range of material, and all volumes contain a further reading and Web sites section that lists a selection of books and Web sites for continued exploration. This selection is also only a sample, offering suggestions of the many exploration opportunities available.

I was once at a conference in which a young student asked a group of professors whether he needed the latest edition of a physics textbook. One professor replied no, because the principles of physics "have not changed in years." This is true for the most part, but it is a testament to the power of physics. Another testament to physics is the astounding number of applications relying on these principles—and these applications continue to expand and change at an exceptionally rapid pace. Steam engines have yielded to the powerful internal combustion engines of race cars and fighter jets, and telephone wires are in the process of yielding to fiber optics, satellite communication, and cell phones. The goal of these books is to encourage the reader to see the relevance of physics in all directions and in every endeavor, at the present time as well as in the past and in the years to come.

 # ACKNOWLEDGMENTS

THANKS GO TO my teachers, many of whom did their best to put up with me and my undisciplined ways. Special thanks go to Drs. George Gerstein, Larry Palmer, and Stanley Schmidt for helping me find my way when I got lost. I also much appreciate the contributions of Jodie Rhodes, who helped launch this project; executive editor Frank K. Darmstadt and the editorial team at Facts On File, Inc., who pushed it along; and the many scientists, educators, and writers who provided some of their time and insight. Thanks most of all go to Elizabeth Kirkland, a super mom with extraordinary powers and a gift for using them wisely.

INTRODUCTION

THE WORD *ELECTRICITY* comes from a Greek word, *elektron,* meaning "amber." Amber is a hard, yellowish substance from plants. Ancient Greeks discovered that rubbing a piece of amber with a wool cloth gave these materials interesting properties, such as the power to draw sparks or to attract and pick up small, lightweight items. The Greeks did not know why this occurred; nor did any of the other ancient civilizations.

Many centuries passed before people understood electricity. Benjamin Franklin showed in the 18th century that lightning is an electrical phenomenon, and only in the late 19th century did Sir Joseph John Thomson discover *electrons,* the small charged particles that are transferred in the amber-wool rubbing and cause these materials to become electrically charged. By that time people had strung many miles of wire to carry electrical power to homes and businesses, since electricity was such a cheap and convenient method of providing energy.

Magnetism followed a parallel course. The ancient Greeks discovered magnetized iron near the city of Magnesia, and its usage included the making of compasses to guide navigators at sea. But the force acting on a compass to make it point toward the north was unknown to these early sailors.

The phenomena of electricity and magnetism—including Earth's *magnetic field,* which acts to align magnetized iron along a north-south direction—came together in the 19th century in the research of Hans Christian Oersted and Michael Faraday. Oersted discovered that electric *currents* produce magnetic fields, and Faraday discovered that changing magnetic fields produce electric currents. There are strong ties that bind electricity and magnetism together.

Electricity and Magnetism examines electricity, magnetism, and the relationship between the two that makes electromagnetism such an important and pervasive component of the modern world. (Light, an electromagnetic phenomenon, has its own volume in the Physics in Our World set and is not discussed here.) There are few pieces of equipment that do not employ electricity to some extent, and this makes the loss of electrical power, such as the blackout that affected the northeastern United States and part of Canada in August 2003, a major catastrophe. Without electric trains and subways, traffic lights, street lamps, and all the other necessities provided by electricity, New York City and other towns came to a screeching halt.

The chapters of *Electricity and Magnetism* introduce the principles of this branch of physics, and then explore their widespread applications. An understanding of electricity and magnetism allowed people to harness these forces more effectively, increasing the already substantial number of electrical devices. Electrical equipment is vital not only to the commuters traveling to and from the office but also to fighter pilots, who soar through the sky in airplanes that are so swift and maneuverable they could not be flown without the help of electronics. Other electrical devices have long been used to store and play music, upgrading in quality from early tin or wax cylinders to modern *compact discs* (CDs). And computers are everywhere, transforming the ways people communicate, conduct business, and read the news—much of which is done electronically or over the Internet. The future holds even more promise of change.

Electricity not only powers modern civilization's technology, it is also the driving force behind much of the human body. This fact, hinted at by Luigi Galvani's finding that frog legs twitch when electrically stimulated, is critical in the biological understanding of the skeletal muscles, heart, and brain, the subjects of the final chapter of *Electricity and Magnetism*. And animals such as certain birds, loggerhead sea turtles, and spiny lobsters can perceive magnetic fields and may use them for navigation and orientation. In its roles in technology, biology, and natural events such as lightning, electromagnetism produces effects that extend throughout the world and affect all its inhabitants.

1

ELECTRICITY

LONG AGO THE Romans described a fish that lived in the Mediterranean Sea and could emit painful barbs or needles, even from a great distance. The people marveled at this fish's ability, because the needles seemed to be invisible—they could be felt but not seen. Roman physicians used the fish to treat painful inflammation of the joints, as well as headaches and other disorders.

This fish, called the torpedo, is an example of an electric fish. All the great civilizations of the ancient world, including the Romans, Egyptians, and Greeks, were familiar with at least one species of electric fish. But none of them had any good idea what source was behind the fish's mysterious power to inflict a potent, numbing sensation at a distance through the water.

Much of today's technology runs on electricity, and although it is not generated in the same way as that of electric fish, the principles are the same. People in the ancient world could not effectively employ this great source of energy because they did not understand the physics of electricity. Yet electricity is quite common, both in modern technology and in nature. Its effects are numerous and widespread. A particularly impressive example can be seen in the sky during a thunderstorm.

Lightning

Lightning comes and goes in an instant, yet it is impossible to ignore. A stroke of lightning is as bright as a million light bulbs and

This photograph captures several lightning strokes during a stormy night. *(NOAA/OAR/ERL/NSSL)*

strong enough to burn or vaporize anything in its path. Lightning is electricity at its most powerful.

People always watched lightning with a sense of fascination and dread, long before lightning was known to be an electrical phenomenon. The earliest theories of lightning had little to do with electricity; the reason for this is that lightning would seem to have nothing in common with electric fish or with the amber and wool of the ancient Greeks, who rubbed these two materials together to produce curious forces of attraction and repulsion. It was not until an American statesman, businessman, and scientist named Benjamin Franklin (1706–90) came along that people realized lightning is related to electricity.

Franklin went out in a thunderstorm in 1752 and performed an experiment with a kite and a key. Franklin reasoned that electricity was due to flowing *charges,* and lightning was caused by electric charges in the atmosphere. In Franklin's experiment, these charges traveled down the damp kite string, and Franklin proved their existence by drawing a spark from a key attached to the string.

Today, physicists know that friction produces electric charges high in the atmosphere. This process occurs when small particles such as water droplets and ice collide or rub against one another. Wind, among other factors, separates these charges, and large electric forces (as given by *Coulomb's law*, described in the sidebar) develop between the ground and the air above. The electric forces are sometimes strong enough to be sensed by people, who may feel their hair standing on end. This is an electrical phenomenon:

Coulomb's Law and Electric Fields

There are two types of electric charges, named positive and negative by Benjamin Franklin. No one is sure exactly what an electric charge is, but charges can easily be identified by their effects on one another. Positive and negative charges attract, but positive charges repel each other, as do negative charges. In electricity, opposites attract and like repels.

The force F that a pair of electric charges Q_1 and Q_2, separated by a distance r, exert on one another is given by the following equation:

$$F = kQ_1Q_2/r^2$$

where k is a constant. This equation is known as Coulomb's law, named after the French physicist Charles Augustin de Coulomb (1736–1806). (The unit of charge is also named after Coulomb. Both of the Qs in the equation represent some number of coulombs.) The equation is identical in form to that of the gravitational force between two masses—replace each Q with an m (representing a mass), and switch the constant k to the gravitational constant G, and the result is the equation of gravitational attraction. Why this is so is one of the most interesting mysteries of nature.

Coulomb's law says that any electric charge exerts a force on other charges in the vicinity. Physicists often find it more convenient to think of the charge as creating a field that they call the *electric field*. The term *electric field* is an abstract way of characterizing the effects felt by charges due to the presence of electrical forces. Physicists use the field concept to help them visualize these forces.

the hairs gather charges of the same sign, which repel with a force strong enough to cause individual hairs to move away from each other, pulling themselves erect in the process.

The atmospheric charges and fields have strong effects. Opposite charges attract and would get together if they could, but something prevents them from doing so: they have no way of reaching one another—until, that is, the forces become so strong that they blaze a path through the air. This is lightning.

A lightning strike is actually a series of strokes, often about four. Movement of charge, called an electric current, brings together charges of opposite sign. Lightning is a flow of electric charges between two objects or regions, which can be two clouds or a cloud and the ground. For a very brief time, the energy produced by the current causes the temperature of the lightning bolt to reach thousands of degrees, and it causes the molecules in the air to give off light. Lightning is so hot that if it strikes the ground it can melt sandy soil, creating a glassy substance called fulgurite.

At any given instant in time, about 2,000 thunderstorms rage across the globe, producing 100 lightning flashes every second. Lightning can spark fires, shatter wood, and damage or even destroy electrical equipment in the vicinity of the strike. It can also kill. About 80 to 100 people each year die from lightning strikes in the United States alone.

Although people now understand that lightning is an electrical phenomenon, hundreds of years ago many people believed that the ringing of bells would ward off lightning. This false belief sent bell ringers climbing up tall buildings during thunderstorms to pull the ropes and ring the bells, and as a consequence hundreds of bell ringers were struck and seriously injured by lightning. This strange and tragic activity persisted until a knowledge of physics indicated that the worst thing to do in an electrical storm is to gain altitude. By Coulomb's law, electrical forces increase when the distance between the charges decreases. The electrical forces created by atmospheric charges can be so strong that they draw sparks from tall objects on the ground—an excellent invitation to a stroke of lightning.

The tendency to hit the tallest object takes some of the chance out of lightning strikes. Lightning is unpredictable to a certain extent, but its preference is for height. This is true in a relative sense, because it is not necessarily the tallest object in the whole storm region that gets struck, but rather the tallest object in the immediate vicinity—anything that sticks out of the crowd. A tree or a house that towers above the rest may be struck, or a golfer standing on a flat golf course may. Skyscrapers are favorite targets. Lightning strikes tall buildings such as the Sears Tower in Chicago and the Empire State Building in New York hundreds of times a year.

Metal provides an excellent path for charges to flow, as described in the following section, and is a favored target. But just about anything will serve; that is why people should not be around pipes, water, or even the telephone during a severe electrical storm. If flowing charges do not have a convenient metallic path, or are blocked in some way, they will often take another path, and this path can include a person's body.

Providing a safe and convenient path for the charges to flow is the idea behind lightning rods. First developed by Benjamin Franklin, a lightning rod offers the easiest pathway for electric charges and, if correctly positioned, is taller than its surroundings. The rod connects with the ground in such a way that if it is struck, it carries the charges harmlessly away to distribute themselves in Earth, which is big enough to hold a lot of them.

Clingy Socks and Jumping Sparks

Clingy socks may not seem to have much in common with lightning, but they do. Both are examples of static electricity.

Any sort of rubbing can separate electrical charges. Rubbing of wool on amber will do so, as will the collisions of atmospheric particles. Socks tumbling together in the clothes dryer can also produce charges, as friction separates the positive and negative charges, and they exert forces on each other, as given by Coulomb's law. These forces are known as electrostatic, because they are electrical and are relatively unchanging, or static—until a discharge occurs. Lightning is the most impressive example, but electrostatic sparks can appear anywhere.

Probably everyone has experienced an electrostatic discharge, in the form of a mild shock. Most often this occurs when walking on a dry carpet and then touching a metallic object, such as a door knob. The charges build up on the person because of the friction between feet or shoes and the carpet. The process transfers small charged particles called electrons, and the person becomes electrically charged. The charges find their way to ground by the path of least *resistance*—usually metal—just as a lightning rod conducts lightning's charges to Earth.

Static electricity is common. After all, friction is quite common in the world—a lot of things rub together. But there is an important factor to be considered: some objects conduct charges better than others. As described in the sidebar, a material that can provide a relatively unimpeded path for electrical charges is a *conductor*.

Conductors and Insulators

All materials allow electrical charges to flow, and everything is, in a sense, an electrical conductor. But some materials are such poor conductors that they are called *insulators*. Rubber, plastic, and wood are good insulators. Tiny charged particles called electrons (which were named after *elektron*, the Greek word for amber) are often the carriers of electricity in solid materials because they tend to be mobile. Electrons are extremely mobile in metals; that is why they are such good conductors.

Resistance is the opposite of conduction. Resistance means that it is hard for electricity to flow. Good conductors like metals have low resistance, whereas good insulators such as most plastics have high resistance. The resistance of a person's skin is between these two extremes, neither an effective conductor nor an effective insulator, though it depends on how wet the person is. Although pure water is not a good conductor of electricity, salty water, such as sweat, is a fair conductor. Salty water contains a lot of *ions*, which are charged particles that can move through the water and carry current. Electricity will readily flow through the skin of a wet person.

Because metal is an excellent conductor of electricity, it is used in lightning rods and electrical wiring. But other objects can conduct electricity. Charges that build up from friction may discharge not in a fiery spark but as a slow, steady draining. Moist air conducts electricity—not nearly as well as metal, but fairly well. The amount of moisture in the air is called humidity, and humid air contains a lot of water vapor. Static electricity is less likely to occur in humid conditions, because the charges that friction separates will quickly meet up by way of the moist air. People dragging their feet across a carpet will not generate much electricity on hot, humid days. Dry conditions are much better.

A few hundred years ago, the only electricity that people had readily available was static electricity. Enterprising people built giant machines to produce charges from friction, and some of the earliest ones used a sphere of metal or glass that someone rubbed with a hand or cloth. Once charged, the sphere could create sparks (which depleted the charge). The charge had to be used shortly after it was generated, because it gradually leaked away via air conduction. Most of today's technology has little use for static electricity and sparks, although there are exceptions. In cars, for example, spark plugs ignite fuel injected into the engine's cylinders.

The problem is that static electricity often shows up anyway. This is rarely a good thing, because sparks can ignite flammable material. One of the most famous disasters caused by static electricity was the crash of the *Hindenburg* at Lakehurst, New Jersey. The *Hindenburg* was a large airship—like a blimp—which on May 6, 1937, arrived at Lakehurst after a flight across the Atlantic Ocean. The airship contained hydrogen gas, a very flammable substance, and was covered in a skin that also proved to be highly combustible. An electrostatic spark set off a terrible blaze, killing 35 of the blimp's passengers and one person on the ground.

Other accidents have occurred, particularly at gasoline stations. Sparks during the refueling of cars have been responsible for numerous fires. Trucks that fill the large underground tanks at gasoline stations also must be careful, because fuel can become charged by friction as it flows at a high velocity through the pipes. If enough charge builds up, there can be an electrostatic spark.

Another problem caused by static electricity and sparking is damage to sensitive electronics. Before touching equipment components, workers make sure that they have no electrostatic charge by first touching a conductor. Any free charges flow off using this path.

Making a Perfect Copy: Copier Machines

Although static electricity can be dangerous and is often nothing but a nuisance, it does have its uses. Spark plugs were mentioned earlier, but they are not the only application of static electricity that is beneficial. Copier machines would not work without static electricity.

To produce a copy, most modern copier machines make a "charged image" of the original document. The process starts with a uniformly charged belt or drum covered with a photoconductor, which is a material sensitive to light. The machine exposes the original document to a bright source of light; the white parts of the document reflect a lot of this light, and the dark parts reflect only a little. This reflected light is focused on the photoconductor, and in places where the light is strong, the charge on the photoconductor vanishes, because the light makes the material conduct and carry away the charges. This does not affect the remaining areas, which correspond to the dark areas of the original, so they continue to be charged. The photoconductor sheet, now charged only in the places corresponding to the dark areas of the original document, contains the charged image.

Next the machine applies ink, or toner, to the charged image to make it become visible. The toner has a charge opposite that of the charged image. *Electrostatic forces* now come into play, for when the toner meets the charged image, it sticks to the charged areas (which correspond to the dark areas of the original), because opposite charges attract. The system removes any excess charge and transfers the toner to a sheet of paper. After an application of heat to fuse the toner onto the paper, out comes the duplicate.

Electrostatic forces also have a few other technological applications, most of which involve coating objects with a sprayed material. Frequently some sort of induction effect is involved.

The induction effect was well known to the ancient Greeks, who noticed that when amber was rubbed with wool these objects would attract small particles. The same experiment can be performed today, by rubbing a plastic object such as a comb on various types of cloth (or hair). When charged, the comb picks up little pieces of paper. The little pieces of paper need not be charged.

The induction effect occurs because all objects are made of molecules, which are themselves composed of little charged particles such as protons (which are positively charged) and electrons (negatively charged). An object is charged when it has an excess of one kind of charge, either positive or negative. It is uncharged, or electrically neutral, if it contains the same quantity of both charges. But if a strongly charged object is placed beside an electrically neutral object, it will attract the charges in the neutral object that have the opposite sign and repel those that have the same sign. As a result, the opposite charges move closer (if they can) and the same-sign charges move in the other direction, as illustrated in the figure.

Although the neutral object still has the same number of charges, they are now distributed in such a way that there is an excess at either end. This distribution is called an electric dipole—

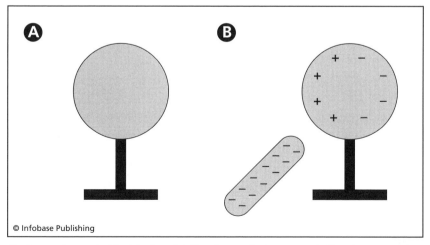

© Infobase Publishing

Placing a charged object in the vicinity of a neutral one repels like charges and attracts opposite charges.

there are two poles, the positive and negative ends of the object. This would not happen without the presence of the electrostatic force from the charged object. Induction creates, or induces, the uneven distribution of charges in the neutral object.

Induction occurs in any object in which charges can move—and that is most objects. In the comb experiment described earlier, the charges on the comb attract small pieces of paper because of induction and the electrostatic force. But why does it only seem to work for small pieces of paper? The answer is provided by Newton's second law of motion, formulated by the British physicist Sir Isaac Newton (1642–1727). This important law of physics says that for a given force, acceleration is inversely proportional to mass. Small objects have small mass and therefore experience larger accelerations for a given force. The induced electrostatic attraction between comb and paper is only strong enough to move the pieces that do not have a lot of mass.

Electrostatic induction is important to crop dusters. Crop dusters spray insecticide on farmland from planes or trucks, and small drops of the material become charged by friction as they leave the nozzle of the spray gun. Because of induction, the drops tend to stick to leaves and stems, not just on top but also underneath and on all sides. The spraying therefore fully covers the plants, so they are better protected from the voracious appetite of insects.

Electrostatic forces can also be used to spread paint evenly on a surface. Tiny droplets of paint, when given the same charge, repel one another. When sprayed on a surface, such as the body of a car, the paint forms a smoother coating—no clumps or bald spots.

Live Wires and Flowing Charges

Static electricity intrigued early physicists, but there was a problem: the experiments could last only a short time. Experimenters charged the metal or glass sphere by rubbing it vigorously, and then after all that effort a little spark could be drawn from it—which could be achieved by placing some conductor close to its vicinity—and the electrical charges flowed in a flash. Then the experiment was over, and it was time to recharge the sphere.

Electric Circuits

In most of its applications, electricity flows in circuits. A circuit is the path taken by the electric charges constituting the current. The figure displays two examples of circuits in a diagram form known as a schematic.

The two circuits in the figure are basic circuits. In the circuit shown on the bottom, the charges flow from a battery to the light bulbs in series, first one bulb and then the next. This is a *series circuit.* The other circuit shows a *parallel circuit,* in which the bulbs are not on the same line but are instead on parallel ones. Series circuits are simpler. Parallel circuits have the advantage that if one of the bulbs burns out and breaks the circuit, the other bulbs will stay lit because there is still a path for charges to flow.

The battery provides a *potential difference,* the *voltage* (the unit of which is the volt, named in honor of Alessandro Volta). The difference in potential that exists across the battery terminals is what drives the charges around the circuit.

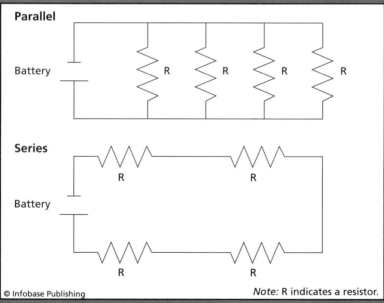

© Infobase Publishing

Note: R indicates a resistor.

The figure illustrates an example of a parallel circuit and a series circuit. Each R is a resistance.

Studying electricity was difficult under such conditions. It was also hard to imagine very many useful applications for electricity. All that rubbing was a bit of a drag, one might say. What was really needed was a source of steady electricity—and a way to control its path.

Then in 1800, an Italian physicist, Alessandro Volta (1745–1827), developed a steady source of electricity. Volta invented the first electric battery. It was not quite like modern batteries, but the idea for both is the same. With Volta's battery, a steady flow of charges became available. Now electricity could really take off.

To control the path of charges, people began building circuits, as described in the sidebar on page 11. The best material with which to make the circuits was obviously metal, a superb electrical conductor.

Not all metals are equally good conductors, however. One of the best is gold. But gold is far too expensive to use for everyday circuits—to wire a house would cost millions of dollars. Because copper is cheap and a relatively good conductor, it is the metal most often used.

Circuits make a complete, closed path for electric charges to flow. Current flows all the way around the loop. If there is an open anywhere in the circuit—a break in the path—a steady current cannot flow.

The charges flow in a circuit like water falling downhill. They move naturally down their gradient; the gradient in this case is an electrical gradient called the potential difference. This is similar to the discharge of static electricity, as separated charges move together again because of electrical forces. But unlike in static electricity, in steady currents the charge must be continuously separated so that it keeps flowing. Separating charges requires work, by friction (as in static electricity), by a battery, or by some other means (described later). As the charges travel around the circuit they move down their electrical gradient, and they must to be "lifted up" again before they will make another trip. This is the job of the battery or other power source in the circuit.

In the late 19th and early 20th centuries, electric power companies formed. Generating electricity at many different locations

Overhead wires are a common sight in cities. *(Kyle Kirkland)*

was not practical, so they built only a few "power plants." To get electricity into homes, people strung metal wires all over the city and countryside to carry the electricity from the power plant to places where it was needed. This is still the way electric power distribution works today, although sometimes the wires are not on poles but instead buried in the ground.

The power lines are part of a tremendously long circuit. Early on, power companies realized that the most efficient way to move electricity over long distances was to use a form called *alternating current* (AC), instead of a constant current (called *direct current* or DC) as from a battery. In AC the charges move back and forth, changing directions periodically.

Efficiency also requires power companies to do something rather dangerous. To minimize losses, the voltage of power lines is usually very high: up to 750,000 volts, which is thousands of times higher than what is needed in homes and businesses. Fewer charges leak out into the surrounding air when the wires carry high voltage. Devices called transformers reduce the voltage to a much lower level—usually about 120 volts in the United States—before it enters a consumer's house or office.

Electricity can be quite dangerous, whether it is flowing through power lines strung high in the air or causing the intense flashes of light in bolts of lightning. Coulomb's law is not a law to be taken lightly—electrical forces can be astonishingly powerful—and hundreds of thousands of volts is a deadly amount. Overhead power lines are not insulated; the conducting wire is not wrapped with an insulator. Buried power cables must be insulated, even though insulating them adds expense, because otherwise too many charges would leak out to the ground (soil is a much better conductor than air). But overhead wires are usually not insulated, and for this reason they are extremely hazardous.

Electricity sometimes fools people. This has always been true, as indicated in the strange bell-ringing theories about warding off lightning. Although scientists such as Coulomb, Franklin, and others discovered the laws of electricity, and engineers designed pathways such as series and parallel circuits in which electricity can flow, charges do not always behave as people might expect. Sometimes, for instance, when people see a bird perched on a power line, they think the wire cannot be dangerous because nothing happens to the bird. But the wire is dangerous, and physics provides the reason why a bird can safely perch there under certain circumstances: the current does not travel through the bird because its body is a relatively high resistance, much higher than the wire itself. So the charges travel the path of least resistance, through the wire, and leave the bird alone.

The problem arises when the bird, or person, touches a live wire and at the same time touches something else, such as the ground. Ground is the lowest potential—this is the farthest downhill that charges can go, and they will always "roll" this far if they can, even if they have to travel through a large resistance. In other words, a high potential difference exists between the wire and ground, high enough to push charges through even a relatively large resistance. If a bird or person touches a power line and ground (or a conductor that leads to ground), electric charges will take this opportunity to roll downhill, much to the discomfort of whoever supplies the path. Each year thousands of birds with large wingspans, such as hawks and eagles, are electrocuted when their wings simultaneously touch a wire and something else, giving charges a pathway to ground.

The best defenses against shock are to observe simple precautions and to understand the physics of electricity. This understanding, gained well after ancient Greeks observed the effects of rubbing amber with wool, led to devices such as copying machines and many others, as described in the following chapters. Because electricity now has more chances to cause an injury than just through natural phenomena such as lightning, a knowledge of physics can be an effective life preserver.

2

MAGNETISM

TRAVELERS CAN USE the Sun and stars to help chart their course, but what about when the sky is cloudy? This is particularly important on the ocean, because sailors have no landmarks to guide them—there is only open sea, which looks the same in all directions. Ships can drift in the wrong direction for miles, and sailors may not even realize they've gone off course.

Getting lost was one of the problems that prevented vessels in ancient times from going very far into the ocean. But the Greeks discovered magnetized iron (lodestone, which is iron oxide) near the city of Magnesia, and people noticed that a free-swinging magnetic rod always aligned itself in a north-south orientation: one end points toward the north and the other end toward the south. No one had any clear idea why this was so, but it worked. This is the compass, the means by which sailors and other travelers could always determine the direction in which they were heading. Although historians do not know exactly when the compass was first used, it was certainly important to sailors in the Mediterranean Sea by the 12th century.

The compass was instrumental in the development of trade. Once shipbuilders learned how to construct stronger, more durable vessels, sailors were able to make long-distance voyages with the aid of the compass. This ushered in the age of discovery, which began in the 1400s and was critical in the development of modern civilization. Europeans came to America, and trade opened up between Europe and Asia.

A compass and map continue to be helpful for finding one's location and maintaining course. *(U.S. Air Force/Master Sgt. Michael Burns)*

The physics of compasses involves magnetism. Magnets and magnetism make their presence felt in many situations, and several advanced technologies use human-fashioned sources of magnetism. But compasses are based on a natural and global source—Earth's magnetic field.

Earth's Magnetic Field

The Earth behaves like a large magnet, as seen in the figure. One *magnetic pole* is located in northern Canada, about 806 miles (1,300 km) from the North Pole (which is the north end of Earth's rotational axis, the "top of the world"). As discussed in the

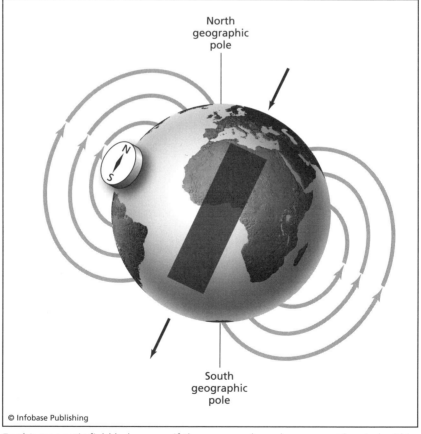

© Infobase Publishing

Earth's magnetic field behaves as if there were a large bar magnet located within the planet, although this is not the actual source of the field.

Magnetic Forces and Fields

Magnets have two poles, called north and south. They are somewhat like the two kinds of electric charge, in that opposite poles attract (north and south poles attract one another, just as positive and negative charges do) and like poles repel, as do like charges. Poles are to magnetism what charges are to electricity, with an important exception: positive and negative charges can be separated, but not magnetic poles. All magnets known to exist have both north and south poles. If a magnet is cut in half, the two separate pieces always form their own north and south poles.

Although no one has ever found convincing evidence for a magnet with a single pole (called a magnetic monopole), some theories in physics suggest that they exist, or at least existed at one time in the history of the universe. If physicists were ever to find magnetic monopoles, that discovery would have a significant impact on a number of advanced theories in physics.

A magnet will pick up a piece of iron or steel (steel is mostly made of iron, with a little carbon) but has much less effect on other metals and especially on nonmetals. Magnetism is due to properties of atoms, which have characteristics similar to those of tiny magnets. The tiny magnets form *magnetic domains* in a piece of matter such as iron, and if the domains all line up in the same direction, then their individual magnitudes add and the material becomes magnetized. If the domains are randomly scattered, then the magnets offset one another, so the object displays little overall magnetism. The material in which the domains line up most readily is iron; that is why iron can be magnetized and even when it is not magnetized is affected by magnets in the vicinity. Other metals, such as nickel and cobalt, can also be magnetized. This property is called *ferromagnetism* because iron is the primary example (*ferro-* is from the Latin word *ferrum,* which means iron). Physicists think of magnets as producing fields of force, called magnetic fields, in the same way that electric charges produce electric fields. The field is an abstract way of describing magnetic forces, useful in visualizing and studying these forces.

Aligning the magnetic domains will magnetize a piece of ferromagnetic material. A person can accomplish this by placing the piece of material in a strong magnetic field or by stroking it with a magnet. The magnet so formed will remain magnetized, though possibly not forever. If something knocks the magnetic domains out of alignment, then the object's magnetism will be lost. Heating or repeatedly striking the magnet will often cause a loss in magnetism.

sidebar on page 19, physicists describe magnetic forces and fields in ways similar to those that apply to electricity. The magnetic field of Earth extends with considerable strength for thousands of miles into space.

Not only is the field responsible for the action of compasses, it also interacts with charged particles, sometimes called cosmic rays, which arrive from space. The force of the magnetic field directs the charged particles toward the magnetic poles. This is what gives people in the extreme northern latitudes some of nature's most fantastic displays of colored light, called the aurora borealis (northern lights). The same also holds true in the south, where the light displays are known as aurora australis (southern lights).

Magnetic compasses experience the force of Earth's magnetic field, which causes them to orient themselves along a north-south direction. The north-south orientation of compasses is the state of least energy, and the one in which an object will naturally come to rest; by analogy to gravity, this is like a valley in which a rolling ball will finally stop. But navigators soon became aware of an odd-

The aurora borealis, shown here in Alaska, presents eerie and spectacular displays of light. *(U.S. Air Force/Senior Airman Joshua Strang)*

ity. They discovered that the compass does not point precisely to the north; instead, it points to somewhere close by. Early sailors were intrigued by this magnetic deviation (which is sometimes called magnetic declination), and ship captains such as Columbus recorded the deviations as they sailed across the seas. Magnetic deviation caused some problems when ships sailed across great distances trying to reach a small target, such as a tiny island in the middle of the ocean. It was less of a problem for Columbus and the sailors who followed him to America, since America is a big place. All the sailors had to do was get into their ship, sail west, and America would appear, sooner or later. But if a sailor wanted to land at a specific part of America, or some such relatively small target, accurate navigation was crucial. Even small errors in a ship's course might result in a miss.

The magnetic deviation arises because the poles of Earth's magnetic field are not located precisely at the North and South Poles. True north, from any point on the globe, is the direction toward the North Pole. But because Earth's magnetic field and not the North Pole is the force acting on the compass, the needle points toward the magnetic pole instead of the North Pole. If a line were drawn to join the north and south magnetic poles of the Earth, it would make an angle of about 11 degrees with the planet's axis of rotation (on which the North and South Poles sit). Although this difference does not cause a large error, navigators have always needed to take it into account.

Another interesting feature about compass directions is that the location of Earth's magnetic poles is not stationary. The poles can move as much as a few miles a year. The poles are also usually not on precisely diametrically opposing positions, as would be expected if Earth's magnetic field were due to a gigantic solid bar magnet embedded in the planet.

Despite these problems, compasses proved to be marvelous tools for navigating the seas, especially in the old wooden ships. Technological progress soon replaced wood with iron and steel, making sturdier ships but also presenting a difficulty with the compass. The iron in a ship's hull and superstructure is usually not strongly magnetic, but even so, it often possesses a weak magnetism—the magnetic domains, though not completely aligned, are not completely random either. The resulting magnetic field will throw off a compass, since Earth's magnetic field is not strong enough to overwhelm the other fields completely. Sailors had to find special places to put their compass to shield it from the ship's "noisy" magnetic fields.

Use of iron ships had other magnetic consequences. During World War II (1939–45), countries transported soldiers and material by sea, such as when the United States moved a large portion of its army to Europe in order to invade German territory. Opponents of course tried to sink each other's ships. Submarines were one method of achieving this, but a cheaper way was to use a large number of mines. These devices would float near the surface of the water and detonate on contact with a passing ship's hull. Floating mines could frequently be avoided because they could be detected by the ship's crew, but then the Germans developed a mine that stayed well underneath the water's surface, yet still exploded when the hull of a ship passed over it. Such a mine was extremely dangerous because it could not be seen until too late.

The puzzle was how the mine exploded at the correct time. Something had to trigger detonation, which was not due to contact with the ship. The solution turned out to be magnetism—a deflection in a compasslike object, caused by the relatively weak magnetism of a nearby ship's hull, set off the mine. The British and American navies had to protect their vessels by creating offsetting magnetic fields to cancel or reduce the magnetic hulls. This was one of the many ways in which the war was a battle of physicists as much as of soldiers.

Since iron is so magnetic, it might seem reasonable to suppose that perhaps Earth's core is one gigantic iron magnet. But explaining Earth's magnetic field is not that easy.

The origin of Earth's magnetic field is still somewhat of a mystery, but physicists believe that it does not simply result from a large piece of iron in the center of the planet. For one thing, Earth's core appears to be too hot for the magnetic domains in its interior to be aligned. The best current theory is that Earth's magnetic field is due to circulating electric currents, an effect that will be described in more detail in a later chapter.

Physicists would very much like to understand Earth's magnetic field more completely, since a better understanding would provide valuable clues to the composition and structure of Earth's vast interior. Scientists are presently unable to make a direct examination of Earth's core by, say, drilling a hole—no one can drill that deep—so everything that can be learned about it here on the surface is most welcome.

An understanding of planetary magnetic fields would also help physicists to understand other planets in the solar system. Jupiter, Saturn, Uranus, and Neptune have much stronger magnetic fields than Earth, but no one yet knows how and why these fields exist. The planet Mercury also has a magnetic field, albeit a weak one.

Perhaps the most interesting and mysterious aspect of Earth's magnetic field is that it is not constant. The particular direction and strength of Earth's magnetic field influence the structure of rocks that solidify from lava, and by studying rocks from past eras scientists have found that the field has varied considerably. Not only that, but flip-flops have occurred: the north and south magnetic poles occasionally reverse. These events seem to occur at irregular intervals. It would be useful to know what causes them, so the next one could be predicted.

Changes in Earth's magnetic field would of course greatly affect compasses. But compasses, once vital to the development of modern civilization, are not nearly as important now. Aiding navigation today is sophisticated equipment such as satellites and gyroscopes. But magnetism has many other applications that make it a crucial part of the present state of technology.

Seeing inside the Body: Magnetic Resonance Imaging

Although Earth's magnetic field is wide-ranging, it is not very strong. It can influence the alignment of molten rocks or a magnetic compass, but most objects are hardly affected.

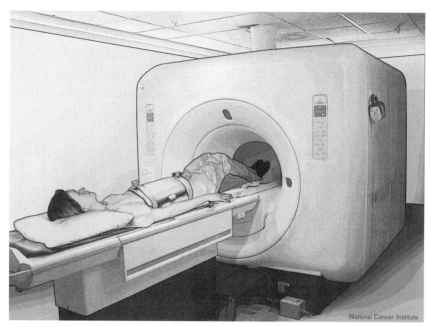

This illustration of an MRI procedure shows a patient sliding into the machine. Images will be taken of the patient's abdomen, which is covered in a pad to improve image quality. *(NCI/Terese Winslow)*

Magnetic fields much stronger than Earth's can be made artificially. By building powerful magnets, scientists and engineers have made a lot of discoveries and developed a number of devices that have had a huge impact on people's lives. One of the most important developments is the use of magnetic fields, along with a certain type of electromagnetic wave, to take pictures of the tissues and organs of the human (and animal) body. The procedure is *magnetic resonance imaging,* or MRI for short.

As X-rays do, MRI provides physicians with a tool to assess a patient's health. But the X-ray is a type of electromagnetic wave that is energetic enough to damage biological tissue if the exposure is too long or too frequent. In most circumstances MRI is safer. X-rays are still used because they excel at showing bones, but MRI gives a much better picture of the "soft" organs.

To have an MRI exam, the patient lies in a very strong magnetic field that is generated by powerful magnets. This field can be up to about 40,000 times stronger than Earth's magnetic field. The MRI machine then applies radio waves to the patient's body; radio waves are electromagnetic waves, as are X-rays, but they are not very energetic and are harmless. (When used in other circumstances, radio waves can carry information—voice and music—as on the radio.)

MRI uses radio waves because this kind of electromagnetic wave affects hydrogen atoms, which the body has in abundance—there are two hydrogen atoms in every water molecule (H_2O), and the human body contains a lot of water (roughly 65–70 percent by weight). The strong magnetic field aligns hydrogen atoms as if they were little compass needles, and the radio waves interfere with this alignment. The MRI machine uses computers to analyze the signals given off by the atoms as they change alignment. Since hydrogen atoms are involved, MRI works best in areas with a lot of water or fat content, such as the brain.

Millions of MRI procedures are performed annually. Images produced by MRI permit doctors to spot diseased tissue and

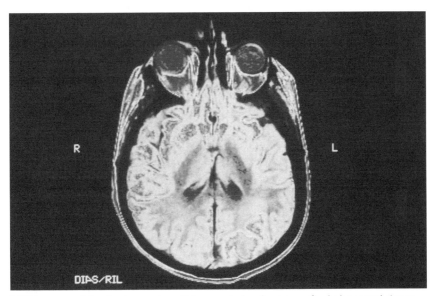

MRI images of the brain, such as this one, help physicians find abnormal tissue. The spot at the back of the brain (bottom of the photograph), in an area known as the occipital lobe, proved to be a cancerous growth. (NCI/Dr. Leon Kaufman)

organs much more easily than they ever could before. These images are particularly useful in finding tumors growing in the nervous system, either in the spinal cord or the brain, and many lives have been saved by their use. Paul C. Lauterbur and Sir Peter Mansfield, scientists who made major contributions to the development of this device, won the Nobel Prize in physiology or medicine in 2003.

But this technology has even more applications. One of the most exciting applications is called fMRI, which stands for *functional magnetic resonance imaging*. An fMRI allows scientists who study the brain to measure the activity of brain cells while the person is awake and thinking. MRI, as described previously, cannot easily do this because it is designed to take a static picture—a still life, a snapshot of the health of the tissue and organs. What is needed is a way of imaging the changes that occur in the brain as a person thinks. This is the "functional" part.

What kind of changes can be observed in the brain as a person thinks? Blood flow is one. Blood carries nutrients and oxygen to the cells of the body, and brain cells are hungrier than most. The brain uses 20 percent of the oxygen in the blood, even though it is only 2 percent of the body's total weight. Here is where fMRI comes in: blood flow increases to brain cells that are especially active. When a person starts thinking, the working part of the brain begins to get a little more "juice" through the blood.

In the earliest fMRI techniques, scientists injected weakly magnetic substances into the bloodstream of the experimental subjects. The machine was able to determine which parts of the brain were more active by using a strong magnetic field (as does MRI) and tracking the blood supply as it flowed to active areas of the brain. Modern fMRI techniques take advantage of a naturally occurring substance in the blood that can be affected by the magnetic fields of the machine. This substance is deoxyhemoglobin, a molecule found in red blood cells. (Hemoglobin is a molecule in red blood cells that contains iron and binds oxygen, carrying it to tissues. Deoxyhemoglobin is hemoglobin without the oxygen bound to it.) Because it is already present in the blood, no injections are required, something that people undergoing an fMRI much appreciate.

By taking images while a person performs various mental tasks or is being subjected to various sensations, scientists can study which part or parts of the brain contribute to behavior. Scientists are discovering clues as to the function of specific parts of the brain. As these techniques gradually improve, a better understanding of the mysteries of how the human brain works will emerge, thanks to magnetism and the ingenuity of physicists and physicians.

Magnetically Levitated Trains

Opposite poles attract, like poles repel, and even objects with a great deal of mass can be affected by a force that is strong enough. This is especially true of magnetically levitated trains, one of the most ambitious projects involving strong magnets.

Magnetic levitation—often called *maglev*—occurs when the magnetic interaction is strong enough to balance the force of gravity. The opposite poles of two magnets repel one another, and if the magnets are placed vertically and the strength of the repulsion is the same as the strength of gravity, the net force is zero. The magnet on top appears to float in air, or levitate.

It generally takes a strong magnet on the bottom and a lightweight magnet on top to do the job. But if the magnets are powerful, even massive objects such as a train can be levitated. It is not easy to levitate something, however, for the same reason that it is not easy to balance a broomstick in the palm of a hand. There are stability issues—things move around and fall over. Magnets that can be quickly adjusted, such as *electromagnets* (described in the following section), are typically used in maglevs.

Plenty of trains already exist that have nothing to do with magnetic levitation, but a maglev train would have certain advantages. One of the major advantages is the elimination of friction that conventional trains encounter as their wheels turn along the railroad tracks. Friction is a force that occurs when two objects rub or slide against one another, and the force tends to oppose motion; it is what causes a person sliding on the floor to come to a stop. The force of friction is necessary to a train's movement because otherwise the wheels would not grip the track, but unintentional friction caused by rubbing among the axles, wheels, and track must be overcome by expending more fuel.

Another reason to develop maglev trains is that they can go very fast, possibly in a way that would be cheaper than other forms of rapid transportation. Maglev trains do not use wheels or axles or other moving parts (at least not when they are going fast), and so they are not limited by mechanical or structural restrictions that these things create. Experimental maglev trains have reached 360 miles per hour (580 km/hr). Maintenance costs should also be lower than those of conventional trains, since the use of fewer moving parts, most of which do not rub together, means less wear and less replacement. Maglev may one day also be involved in launching spacecraft, helping to boost vehicles to the high speed necessary to go into orbit or escape Earth entirely.

Magnetic fields not only levitate but also propel maglev trains. Propulsion occurs because the magnetic field changes around the

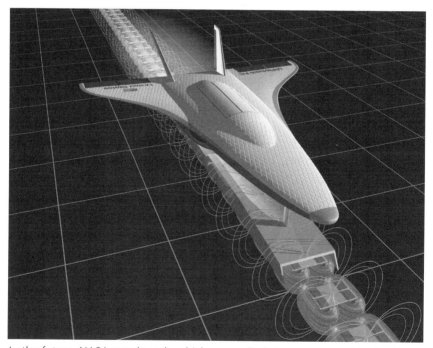

In the future, NASA may launch vehicles propelled along a magnetic levitation system. *(NASA)*

moving train, attracting the train to the area ahead or repelling it from the area behind (or both). Some maglev trains ride waves in a magnetic field almost the way a surfer rides an ocean wave.

But maglev trains are more talked about than ridden. In most designs, the guide way—the path that provides the magnetic fields to levitate and propel the train—is expensive. In contrast to conventional trains, in which the track is fairly cheap but the locomotives and cars are costly, maglev trains require a large initial investment to build the pathway along which the train moves. The expense is great enough to discourage or even prohibit construction plans. Many maglev projects have been proposed and discussed in the United States and several other countries, but only a few routes in China and Germany are presently in operation or will be soon.

Magnetism in railways and trains still has a lot of unfulfilled promise. This is in distinct contrast to magnetic compasses, which have more or less played out their promise and have been mostly replaced by other, improved devices. Yet magnetism remains a remarkable influence on people's lives and in the world because of its tremendous number of odd and unique effects. Whether at work in a compass needle pointing toward the north or in the imaging of the brain as it thinks, magnetism is a highly significant phenomenon.

3

ELECTROMAGNETISM

FOR MANY YEARS physicists considered electricity and magnetism to be two separate, distinct phenomena. There were some similarities in the behavior of magnetic poles and electric charges, but there seemed to be nothing to suggest that electricity and magnetism were strongly related. But then in 1820 the Danish physicist Hans Oersted (1777–1851) made an astonishing discovery: Current flowing through a conductor produces a magnetic field.

The relationship between electricity and magnetism is an example of how seemingly unrelated events or processes are actually connected. Such a connection unifies the concepts and laws of physics and makes them simpler and more powerful, since a group of related laws is a lot easier to understand than a group of unrelated ones. Just as Newton's law of universal gravitation explained both the fall of an apple and the orbit of the Moon, the relationship between electricity and magnetism shows that the physical laws governing the universe are simpler and more elegant than they appear at first. Much research in physics today is motivated by the desire to connect and unite many, or even all, of the laws of physics into one simple rule or formula.

Electromagnetism is a consequence of the properties and interactions of electric charges, by which magnetic fields arise. Many applications of this branch of physics exist in the world today.

Electromagnets

Putting electric charges in motion turns out to be a good way of not only powering an electrical circuit, but also producing a magnetic field. Charges in motion constitute a current, which is

Electric Currents and Magnetic Fields

A current flowing through a straight wire produces a magnetic field with a circular geometry, wrapping itself around the wire. This is different from the magnetic field of a bar magnet, which curves around from pole to pole, as shown in part a) of the diagram.

A current-carrying conductor can produce a magnetic field like that of a bar magnet if the wire is shaped in a certain way. The shape is in the form of a coil, with some number of winding turns, and is critical for a lot of applications of electromagnetism. The turns of wire cannot touch one another, since contact would create a "short" path that would not carry the charges all the way through the coil. If the charges bypass most of the coil, the current is the same as that of a straight conductor. Another way of preventing this from happening is to insulate the wire, so that the turns can be bunched together yet still not suffer from any short circuits. Coils find use in a large number of devices, and they produce magnetic fields as shown in part b) of the diagram.

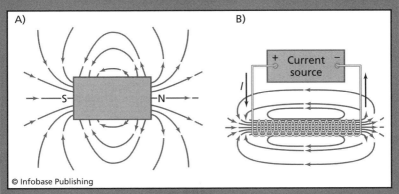

© Infobase Publishing

A current-carrying coil of wire (B) has a magnetic field similar to a bar magnet (A).

the reason Oersted made his discovery. The sidebar on page 31 explores the relation between currents and magnetic fields.

The generation of magnetic fields by electric currents has many uses. This is true even though magnets are already readily available from sources such as iron. The reason has to do with controlling the magnetism, which in the case of electric currents means controlling the current.

Although it is not obvious, iron's magnetization is also due to electricity. The magnetic domains that line up to produce magnets are composed of atoms, and atoms have negatively charged electrons circling their nucleus. This is a charge in motion. A current flowing in a copper wire consists of a huge number of slowly moving electrons, which, as Oersted found out, produces a magnetic field. Atoms also produce tiny magnetic fields, although instead of being caused by a bunch of electrons moving through a wire, this field is due to a hard-working electron zipping around the nucleus. In ferromagnetic materials such as iron, the atomic magnetic fields can add together if they are aligned. If they are not aligned they simply cancel each other out, as waves that interfere with one another do. This is why nonferric materials have little magnetism—they have hard-working atomic electrons but the magnetic domains do not align properly.

An iron magnet is magnetic because of the movement of electric charges, though on the atomic level. But an atomic electron does not have an off switch, and the field of "permanent" magnets such as magnetized iron is difficult to turn on and off. In reality, they are not necessarily permanent, because they can be demagnetized by shaking the domains out of alignment. As mentioned earlier, a large application of heat will do this, as will a series of solid taps with a hammer.

But to turn a magnetic field on and off, it would be far easier to flip a switch. This can be done in magnets produced by currents flowing in a conductor. In this case, all that is necessary is to shut off the current. Such magnets are called electromagnets.

Powerful electromagnets are often used in recycling centers and junkyards to separate reusable scrap metal. The strong magnetic field attracts and picks up pieces of iron and steel, pulling them out of a jumbled heap. The magnet, with the scrap metal attached, moves over a container, and when the operator switches off the magnet, the force of attraction disappears and the metal falls into the bin.

Electromagnets provide control over when and how much of a magnetic field is applied. This is necessary, for example, in the magnetically levitated trains discussed in the previous chapter. Currents and magnetic fields are important in a lot of other ways and find frequent employment in the hands of police and security personnel.

Finding a Concealed Weapon: Metal Detectors

Searching for something is usually as easy as using the eyes to look around. But there are situations when it is convenient to give natural vision a little help. This is especially true when someone is hiding a dangerous weapon and is intent on keeping it concealed.

Many weapons are made of metal, because metals are strong enough to deliver or withstand powerful forces. But metal is also a good conductor of electricity, and an electric current produces a magnetic field. This effect can be used to detect a piece of metal, even if it is concealed.

Before the metal can be detected, though, an electric current must flow in the metal. Since a person who is concealing the weapon is not likely to have it hooked up to a circuit, this requirement might seem to be an insurmountable problem. But it is not, because all one needs to induce an electric current is a magnetic field—and relative motion.

If a metallic conductor moves in a magnetic field (or a magnetic field moves, or changes, in the presence of a stationary metallic conductor), small currents are generated in the conductor. This process is called *electromagnetic induction*. (It is stated by *Faraday's law*, as described in the sidebar on page 34.) If the conductor forms part of a circuit, a current will flow just as if there were a battery or some other power source attached. In other circumstances, when the conductor is simply a block of metal, the

Faraday's Law

Michael Faraday (1791–1867) was a brilliant British physicist who got his start in a humble way, as a laboratory assistant. Although he lacked formal education, Faraday had tenacious curiosity and innate intelligence that drove him to make many important discoveries. One of the most important occurred when Faraday studied the work of Hans Oersted. Since electricity produces magnetism, Faraday wondered if magnetism could produce electricity. He showed that this was true, and electromagnetic induction is described by Faraday's law. A changing magnetic field creates an electric field in a nearby conductor, which gives a push to the conductor's mobile electrons. Thus the changing magnetic field "induces" a current.

The induced current will of course produce a magnetic field itself. But the orientation of the magnetic field of the induced current will not be attracted to the changing magnetic field that created it. The magnetic field created in the conductor is repelled by its creator, because the closest poles are of the same kind.

currents swirl around the inside. These currents are sometimes referred to as eddy currents.

As all charges in motion do, eddy currents generate a magnetic field. Therefore all that is needed to detect a chunk of metal is to have it pass through a strong magnetic field. The motion through the magnetic field induces eddy currents that, in turn, produce their own magnetic field, and this can be sensed by the circuitry of the metal detector. The metal detector produces a strong magnetic field and then "listens" for a response.

The metal detectors in airports and elsewhere are often configured as archways, through which people must pass to enter the secure area. Sometimes hand-held metal detectors called wands are also used. The same concept is being applied in both situations: magnetic fields probe for weapons made of metal. Soldiers also use metal detectors to search for weapons buried in the ground.

An inconvenience of this process occurs when metal other than weapons triggers the detector. Keys, coins, and even metal

Metal detectors help soldiers find buried weapons in Iraq. *(U.S. Army/Staff Sgt. Kevin Moses Sr.)*

implanted in the body (such as plates and screws to help fractures heal) will also set off the alarm. Exactly how much metal will trigger an alarm depends on the sensitivity of the detector (such as the strength of the metal detector's magnetic field) and the type of the metal. Ferrous metals yield a stronger magnetic field than nonferrous metals, and so they are more easily detected.

Of course weapons are not the only objects that people hunt with metal detectors. Some people use metal detectors to find treasure—coins, jewelry, and relics—that is buried near the surface of the soil.

Devices that operate much as metal detectors do can also be used in many other ways. Traffic detectors that sense the presence of automobiles work in a similar fashion. Engineers place current-carrying wire coils underneath the street, and the passing of a car, which contains a significant amount of metal (especially iron), changes the magnetic field of the coils. These changes indicate that a car is nearby.

Tape Recorders and Computer Disks

The notion that magnetic fields can be used to store information and record or play back speech and music dates back to the 19th century. But the technology to do this was not easily achieved. Scientists and engineers developed magnetic tapes in the 1930s and 1940s, but these tapes were noisy and not widely used. The problem was that electromagnetic technology lacked sophistication—it was awkward and unreliable. Speech and music recordings at the time were more likely to be stored in the grooves of vinyl records called phonographs.

The development of reliable and inexpensive magnetic tape recorders came about in the 1960s. One of the chief motivations was the desire to listen to recorded music in cars (phonograph players would not work very well because of the motion and vibration). Engineers designed the eight-track cartridge to suit this purpose, but compact cassette tapes quickly replaced eight-track cartridges. Cassettes soon spread not only to car stereos but many other applications (and have only recently been themselves replaced, for most purposes, by compact discs).

Magnetic tapes are made with a flexible material coated with a thin layer of magnetic particles, such as compounds containing iron, cobalt, nickel—ferromagnetic materials. The device that writes and reads the information, called the head, is a miniature electromagnet containing a coil of wire wrapped around a small magnet.

First, a microphone transforms sound to be recorded into an electric current, which will be used to magnetize the particles on the tape in a certain way. A current flowing through the coil in the head creates a magnetic field, aligning the poles of the magnetic particles as the tape moves past. The figure shows an example of this kind of alignment. The amount of current flowing through the coil determines the strength of the coil's magnetic field and the number of magnetic particles that are affected; the direction

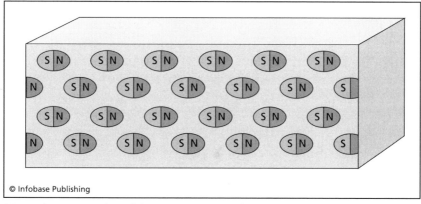

© Infobase Publishing

Magnetic tape consists of tiny magnetic particles whose orientation represents the recorded information.

of current determines the direction of the pole alignment (for instance, whether the north pole of the particles is left or right). Any sound can be stored in the number and alignment of tiny magnetic particles embedded in the tape.

Playback occurs when the magnetized tape passes by the head. By electromagnetic induction, this produces a small current in the coil, proportional to the number of magnetized particles. The machine sends the electric signal to a speaker in order to transform it from current back to sound.

A serious problem with magnetic tape is that strong magnetic fields can erase the recordings by destroying the alignment of the particles. Magnetic fields such as those that surround power transformers will do this, as one young airman in the U.S. Air Force once discovered when he placed a tape full of important military information near a transformer and soon thereafter found, to his dismay, that all the information had disappeared. (This young airman became much wiser in his later years, by the way, and is the author of this book.)

Computer disks also store information in the pole orientation of small magnetic particles. In computers, however, the information is usually stored to suit the binary language of these machines. Computers store and operate with information called data that are represented by long strings of 1s or 0s; each 1 or 0 is one data bit. (Data coded in this way are *digital* data; they are discussed in more detail in a later chapter.) Magnetic storage is excellent for storing strings of 1s and 0s, with each bit represented by a tiny magnet (or small group of magnets). The magnet's north pole may be to the right to represent a 1, or to the left to represent a 0. The digital data stored on computer disks are coded as the orientation of a huge number of magnetic poles. In computer terms, one byte is eight bits; the storage capacity of computer disks is given in megabytes (millions of bytes), gigabytes (billions), or terabytes (trillions).

Disks are similar to magnetic tape in that they possess a coating of a magnetic substance, although disks usually have a rigid backbone. The substance can be a thin film of iron oxide or perhaps a cobalt alloy. Computers do all manner of jobs previously requiring a lot of human effort and have truly revolutionized all aspects of human activity. One of the reasons why is that their disks store so much information cheaply and reliably. Disk storage was not always so cheap: in the mid-1950s, a five-megabyte disk drive cost about $50,000, whereas today an 80-gigabyte disk goes for less than $100—that is, 16,000 times more storage capacity at a tiny fraction of the cost. Only after computers and disks became economical did they find widespread applications.

Banking on Magnetism: Credit Cards and Debit Cards

Storage of information by magnetic means transformed not only the music and computer business. It transformed all business.

Up until the 1960s, virtually all business transactions were done with paper, most of it in the form of cash or checks. Today, when money changes hands, often it does so by way of bank cards— plastic cards, issued by a bank or credit company, which usually have a magnetic strip on the back. Cards are also used to operate laundry machines, parking meters, copiers, and other devices, although many of these cards do not have magnetic strips but instead employ electronic circuits, as described in chapter 6.

Money cards can be used for many devices today, such as this parking meter in Philadelphia. *(Kyle Kirkland)*

Information is stored and retrieved on the magnetic strip in much the same way that data are stored on a computer disk. But magnetic strips usually hold a small amount of data compared to disks—normally about 200 bytes, consisting of the card number, the owner's name, and the card's expiration date. This information identifies the user and the account that are to participate in the transaction.

Cards may be used for credit—which means the money is being borrowed—or debit, which means the system takes the money to pay for the goods or services directly from the buyer's account. Either way, the transaction must be conducted by a computer. When the owner swipes his or her card through a "reader," the machine reads the card's data and passes this information, along with the amount of payment, to a computer. Typically this process involves computers that are connected via a network of computers belonging to the bank or credit card company that issued the card. The system approves and records the transaction, finalizing the deal.

Automation based on bank cards has eliminated the need for bank tellers for many basic transactions. Not long ago a person who needed cash was forced to visit his or her bank during business hours and present a check or a withdrawal slip to a teller. These days, automatic teller machines (ATMs) are everywhere, providing access to bank accounts 24 hours a day, every day of the year.

But the system is not without an occasional glitch. Magnetism writes the data on bank cards, and magnetism can erase it, too. Earth's magnetic field is present everywhere, but fortunately it is not strong enough to wipe a card. Floating around in the modern technological world, however, are magnetic fields that are quite a bit stronger than Earth's.

Some time ago the author of this book was lucky enough to tour a hospital along with a number of other visitors. The hospital staff allowed visitors to roam freely and watch some of the impressive medical devices. One of these was an MRI machine, which, as discussed in an earlier section, generates extremely powerful magnetic fields. The author, who as the aforementioned young airman had accidentally erased a tape by placing it near a strong magnetic field, took the precaution of removing the bank cards from his wallet before getting close to the MRI machine. Other people, evidently, did not. As a result, using their bank cards after the tour proved to be a frustrating experience. The machine rejected the transaction and spat out the card with a terse message: "Invalid data."

4

ELECTRICAL POWER

NATURE PROVIDES ELECTRICITY in the form of thunderstorms and electrostatic sparks, which are sometimes useful and sometimes not. Much more useful are the power outlets in homes and businesses, providing a convenient source of energy. Many experts believe electrical power is the most vital component of modern civilization. Considering the number of devices that run on electricity—almost everything, these days—this would not appear to be an exaggeration.

Did the early physicists who worked out an understanding of electricity know what their efforts would eventually accomplish? They probably did not, for most of them performed their research for the love of it. But once people "tamed" the physics of electricity, then at least some of it could be put into a "bottle," ready to be deliver energy on demand. For electricity, the first such bottle was a battery.

Batteries and Direct Current

A battery is one of the most common sources of electricity. It produces direct current (DC) which is current that flows in only one direction. Batteries operate flashlights, cameras, cell phones, watches, hearing aids, cars, and more. Most portable devices that people use today get power from a battery of one kind or another.

Batteries are manufactured in different shapes and sizes, but all of them operate in the same general way. Inside a battery, a chemical reaction produces a potential difference across the battery's two terminals. When the battery connects to a circuit or conductor, it provides the force to put charges in motion. (Usually the conductor is metal, in which case the moving charge is the negatively charged electron. In other cases, both positive and negative charges move in the conductor. But as far as the work done by electricity, it does not matter whether the movement is negative or positive charge, or both.)

One of the most common batteries is the 1.5-volt battery, such as those used in flashlights. Most of these batteries run on either a zinc and carbon reaction or a zinc and manganese oxide reaction. The voltage produced by these chemical reactions happens to be 1.5 volts; the amount of voltage is not something that the manufacturing selects, but is instead due to the nature of the reaction. To get a higher voltage while still using this same chemical reaction, battery manufacturers can put several batteries, or "cells," in series, as shown in the figure. By placing six 1.5-volt cells in series, a manufacturer can produce a nine-volt battery. (Voltage in a series configuration adds.)

The chemistry underlying the battery's source of power can be complicated, although the effect is simple. A zinc/manganese oxide

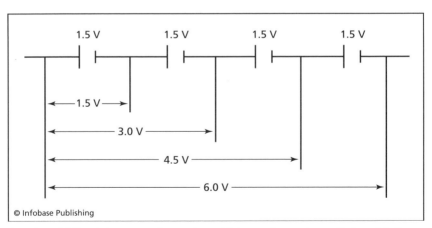

© Infobase Publishing

A series of 1.5-volt battery cells produces higher voltages, in multiples of 1.5 volts.

cell, for example, resembles a slow and controlled form of combustion. Just as people burn wood for heat, these batteries "burn" zinc to generate electricity.

Inventors originally developed batteries because of the need for a steady source of electricity. The 1.5 volts from a flashlight battery stays constant over time—if it fluctuated, the light would periodically dim and brighten. Batteries do have a lifetime, of course, and eventually they lose their ability to generate electricity. This happens when the chemical reaction uses up all of its energy, similarly to the way a car expends all of its gasoline and quits running. The chemical reactions usually only proceed when the battery is working (that is, when it is hooked into a circuit and producing current); that is fortunate, because it means that when the battery is sitting on the shelf, it is not losing much of its power. (It loses some, but not nearly as much as it does when it powers a circuit.)

Even when the chemical reaction becomes exhausted, some batteries can be reused. This process is called recharging, but it can occur only if the reaction is reversible. Any chemical reaction transforms some chemicals into others; for instance, A and B react to form C and D. In the reverse reaction, C and D react to form A and B. All chemical reactions are reversible to some extent, but it is practically impossible to get some reactions to proceed in the reverse direction at a high enough rate. If this is the case, then the battery is not rechargeable.

But in a battery that uses reversible reactions, the original chemicals can be re-formed and the battery's electrical "life" restored. Doing so requires running the reaction in reverse. This means that since the original reaction produced electricity, the reverse reaction will consume it. In a rechargeable battery, recharging sends an electric current through the battery's terminal in a direction opposite its normal flow. But only in a rechargeable battery will this work; trying to do this with a nonrechargeable battery not only is a waste of time but can be risky as well, depending on the battery type. The result might be an exploding battery.

Although rechargeable batteries are available, manufacturers still make batteries that are nonrechargeable. Economics is the reason, because some of the cheaper reactions are not reversible but make usable, inexpensive batteries.

Once Volta invented the first battery in 1800, physicists became interested in understanding and describing the electrical circuits that people built. At first they had no way of measuring current

Ohm's Law

Despite its name, Ohm's law is not really a law: not all materials obey it, and for many materials that do, it is obeyed only within certain limits. Even so, this relationship is extremely useful and the formula is beautifully simple, relating voltage V, resistance R, and current I:

$$V = IR.$$

Voltage is a potential difference—the difference in electrical potential between two points. Anytime someone measures voltage, there are always two points involved. If one point is at a higher potential, then this means a charge will be pushed to the lower potential if a conductor is placed between those points. In other words, a current will flow downhill, from high to low potential.

Resistance impedes the flow of current. Rearranging Ohm's law shows that current = voltage/resistance. For a given voltage, a higher resistance means a lower current. A lower resistance draws more current. If the resistance is practically zero, then a dangerous amount of current flows—this is a short circuit.

A plot of Ohm's law, as shown in the figure, is simple. Plotting voltage (the vertical axis) versus current (the horizontal axis) produces a straight line. The slope of this line equals the resistance.

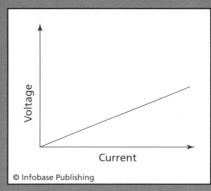

© Infobase Publishing

Ohm's law says that the relationship between voltage and current is linear: voltage equals the product of resistance and current.

except to test it with their fingers, or—as many of them did—to use their tongue, a body part that is extremely sensitive to current. Fortunately, people soon developed equipment called voltmeters, ammeters, and ohmmeters that measured the properties of electrical circuits without requiring physicists to put their life and limbs (and tongues) at risk. Then the German physicist Georg Ohm (1787–1854) discovered a simple formula relating these properties that is widely used today: the voltage across any two points in a circuit is equal to the resistance multiplied by the current. The sidebar on page 44 discusses *Ohm's law* in more detail.

An analysis of electrical circuits shows some of the properties required of power sources. A large resistance requires a lot of voltage to drive charges around the circuit. Ohm's law says that if the resistance is doubled, the current in the circuit is halved for a given battery.

Many of the devices people would like to use require a lot of electricity to operate. Batteries are fine for flashlights, watches, and other relatively simple devices that do not consume a lot of power, but they are not sufficient for many other devices. Portable computers such as laptops, which run on batteries, can only function for relatively small periods without recharging. Engineers often complain that portable devices such as laptops, cell phones, and digital cameras are constrained by a lack of adequate power sources. These devices could have many more functions if only some source could supply enough electricity to run them, but the batteries that exist today are not able to provide enough current to do the job. The lack of a strong enough battery has also severely hampered the development of electric cars.

Physicists are working on this problem. Researchers are looking at many different types of chemical reactions and other sources of energy, such as those involving molecular forces. Experimenters have built small batteries the size of pencil tips, which could power extremely small devices. The goal is to pack as powerful a source of electricity as possible into a small size. If physicists succeed, the cell phones, cameras, and computers that people carry around will soon become even more numerous and achieve greater capabilities.

Power Companies and Alternating Current

Direct current from batteries is not the only way of producing electricity. Most of the electricity generated in the United States and the rest of the world is made by an entirely different process. The electric power companies produce and distribute current by making excellent use of the physics of electromagnetic induction.

Faraday's law says that a changing magnetic field induces an electric current in a conductor, and this is how power companies generate electricity. For example, spinning a loop of wire in the presence of a strong magnetic field produces a current, and if the loop forms part of a circuit, the current flows out through the wires.

According to the laws of electromagnetic induction, all that is required for electricity generation is a changing magnetic field. This could be done by varying the strength of the magnetic field or, as in the example given above, by spinning a wire loop in a constant magnetic field. Although the magnetic field stays the same

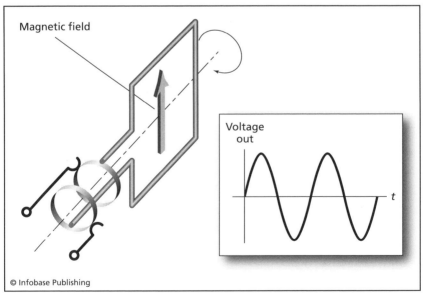

A rotating loop in a magnetic field produces alternating current that varies as a sine wave.

in this case, the loop experiences a varying strength as it rotates because its orientation changes with respect to the field. One way of envisioning this is to picture the magnetic field as a set of parallel lines of force; as the loop of wire turns, it cuts the lines of force, and this is what pushes the electric charges around the circuit (in other words, it "induces" the charges to move, producing a current). The figure gives an illustration.

Electricity is a form of energy and can do work—the ability to do work, in the sense of moving an object with some kind of force, is the definition of energy. But electrical energy is not free, since energy is needed to produce the relative motion between the magnetic field and the conductor. Electricity generation is a type of energy transformation, allowed by the law of conservation of energy, which states that energy cannot be created or destroyed. Mechanical energy, in the form of a rotating loop of wire, transforms into electrical energy.

The current produced by power companies using electromagnetic induction is not direct current (DC); it is alternating current (AC). In DC, the current flows at a constant rate in one direction, but in AC it varies over time, periodically reversing direction. A plot of AC over time would look like a wave, and it is often a special type of wave called a sine wave, a function shown in the figure on page 46. In the United States, the AC produced by power companies reverses at a rate of 60 times a second. The unit for frequency is *hertz*, so in the United States the electric power is said to operate at 60 hertz. The frequency is 50 hertz in Europe.

AC is the natural result of spinning a loop of wire in a magnetic field, as the current varies in a sinusoidal (sine-wave) manner. Since the rest of the circuit does not move, the contact between it and the rotating loop must slide. This contact occurs in junctions called slip rings, in which a rotating wire continues to touch a conductor by sliding along a ringed surface.

There are several ways of turning AC into DC, and DC would seem to be simpler. How come power companies use AC and not DC? Physics provides the answer. Electricity must be efficiently and safely transmitted and distributed, as the power companies have only a small number of places to generate electricity, and they must find some way of delivering the electricity to consumers who may be far removed from the generators. One of the major problems with DC is that there is no way to do this efficiently and safely. With AC, there is a relatively easy way, thanks to devices called transformers.

A transformer is another excellent example of the laws of physics in action. As seen in the figure, a transformer consists of two coils of separate wire, with an iron core running between them. The coils are on separate circuits and are not in physical contact, so current does not transfer directly between them. Instead, electromagnetic induction transfers the current.

Current flowing through a wire produces a magnetic field, and alternating current flowing down one coil of the transformer, called the primary coil (or winding), produces an alternating magnetic field. This field magnetizes an iron core, thereby influencing the second coil of the transformer (called the secondary coil, or winding). The changing magnetic field produces a current in the

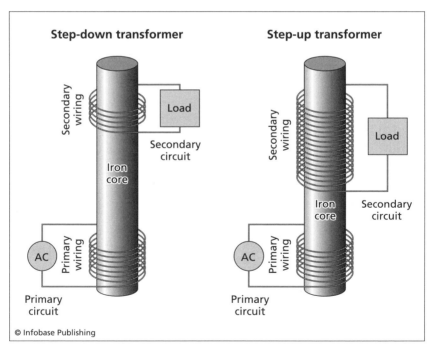

A step-down transformer (left) and a step-up transformer (right)

secondary coil by electromagnetic induction. As if by magic, the primary coil transfers current to the secondary coil, although they remain separate. (But no magic is involved, only physics.)

The amount of current induced in the secondary coil depends on the amount of current in the primary coil and the number of turns in the coils. Having a higher number of turns of the wire around the magnetic core allows the field to do more work on the charges, and the voltage generated in the secondary coil is proportional to the number of turns. Giving the secondary coil more turns than the primary means that the voltage is higher in the secondary than in the primary; fewer turns means a lower voltage. In this way, AC voltages can be "stepped-up" or "stepped-down" by transformers, depending on the relative number of turns in the primary and secondary coils.

This will not work with DC because the field must be changing. Transferring DC would need a direct link, so everything would have to be hooked together. Unpleasant events can happen when everything is connected together, because if something goes wrong in any part of the circuit, the whole neighborhood is in trouble. This only happens in AC when a major line fails—an event that occurs often enough—but there are fewer problems in AC than DC.

Both stepping-up and stepping-down are necessary. The power company's generators may produce electricity at 10,000 volts, but energy, to be transported efficiently along power lines, needs to be increased to 300,000 volts or more. (AC voltage changes periodically, so the values are often given in terms of DC equivalent voltages.) But this voltage is too dangerous to be used in everyday circuits and small devices, so it must be stepped-down before it reaches homes and businesses. The stepped-down level in the United States is about 120 volts.

Power companies bill their customers on the basis of not voltage or current but both, multiplied together. The voltage in a circuit multiplied by the current equals what physicists call power: energy used per unit of time. Power companies calculate electric bills by multiplying the amount of power a customer uses with the amount of time this power is used, and the result of the calculation is the number of kilowatt-hours (power in kilowatts and

Transformers convert the high voltage of the power company's lines into a lower, safer voltage for homes and businesses. *(Kyle Kirkland)*

time in hours). The watt is a small unit of power, equal to about 0.00134 horsepower; the kilowatt, equal to 1,000 watts, is a more convenient unit.

Although transforming up to high voltages for power lines is efficient, it is disconcerting, and not just in terms of the hazard of electric shock. High voltage produces electric and magnetic fields (EMFs) that project a considerable distance from the lines. There is some worry that these fields may cause health problems for people who live nearby. Some medical studies have suggested that living near an EMF source can slightly increase the risk of certain types of health problems such as cancer. But other studies have failed to find such a link. At the present time, most scientists feel that the risk is extremely low if it exists at all, but further research is ongoing.

The Importance of Being Grounded

Wherever electricity is, there is also the danger of electric shock. Electric shock kills hundreds of people every year, particularly those who have to work around high-voltage power lines, such as personnel employed by utility companies.

It is their good fortune that people are not usually effective electrical conductors. As mentioned earlier, the skin of a person, when dry, has a great deal of resistance to the flow of current. According to Ohm's law, the higher the resistance, the less the current. This is good because it is current—the flow of charges—that hurts people, causing burns due to excessive heating and quite possibly also causing disruptions in the heart rhythm (which is generated by the natural electricity of the body, as described in a later chapter).

But if the voltage is high enough, by Ohm's law the current will also be high, even for large resistances. Caution is always necessary around electricity and electrical equipment, especially power lines.

One common safety feature on electrical appliances is the third prong on the power cord. The ground prong, as it is often called, protrudes farther than the other two prongs. It does not play a role in getting power to the appliance, and some equipment, including many older models, does not have a ground prong on the power cord. The ground prong's function is to carry away any charges that might accumulate on the appliance. This could occur, for example, if a wire carrying a lot of current accidentally made contact with the case or cover of the appliance. This is a short circuit—charges are flowing along a path they were not meant to travel. If the exterior of the appliance is a conductor (and most of them are, because they are metal), then it takes on the same potential as the wire. A wire carrying power into the appliance typically has a high voltage, and if a short circuit occurs, then the surface of the appliance will also be at a high potential.

Such situations are exceptionally dangerous. Because the appliance's cover is at a high potential, current will flow from the material if there is a path. A person touching the appliance, or even just brushing up against it, will provide part or all of that path and receive a severe shock because of the current that flows through the body.

But if the charges have an alternative path that is much more favorable to current—a smaller resistance, in other words—then this path will be followed instead. People are conductors, but not in general good ones, and metal is much better. This is the function of the ground prong, for it is in contact with the metal exterior of the appliance. The ground prong sticks out farther than the other prongs because it should be the first thing to make contact. An alternative pathway should already be in place before any power is applied.

The ground prong connects to what is called an electrical ground. An electrical ground is at zero potential and is essentially a large conductor that soaks up charges. Earth is the biggest and best electrical ground, and almost all buildings have a metal pole or rod driven deep into the ground. (It is not hard to imagine how electrical grounds got their name.) Everything that can accidentally accumulate charge, and thus become an electrical hazard, connects with this ground, just as the ground prong connects the metal casing of an appliance to ground. Lightning rods are also grounded.

Charges seek ground wherever they can find a path. This is the equivalent of water flowing down hill—it is something that happens naturally. Or, as physicists like to say, it is energetically favorable. If there is no path, there is no current. The floors of electricians' shops are usually covered with thick, insulating mats, in order to keep the workers electrically isolated from ground. And, of course, alternative paths are provided, and equipment is grounded. The critical aspect of working around dangerously high voltages is never to become part of a path to ground.

Blackouts and Brownouts

New York City on August 14, 2003, was an interesting place to be. Most of the electrical power had been cut off—there was a blackout.

Affecting more than 50 million people, the blackout of 2003 was the most extensive ever experienced in North America up to that date. Part or all of eight states in the northeastern United States and the province of Ontario in Canada were without power, except small backup generators and batteries, for hours. Even after power was restored it took several days for conditions to get back to normal.

Numerous other blackouts have occurred throughout the United States and the rest of the world. The causes are varied and include human error and accidents. But the reason that blackouts can happen in the first place involves the physics underlying the generation and distribution of electricity.

Electricity is not easily stored. Batteries can do it, but only small amounts of power can be stored in this way. The power required by many everyday appliances such as air conditioners and hot water heaters must be served by generators. Since electricity cannot easily be put into a battery or placed on a shelf for use as needed, it must be generated as it is consumed. This necessity leads to a problem, for there must always be a balance between generation and usage.

Maintaining this balance is difficult for power companies because usage varies. There is much more of a demand, for instance, on hot summer days, because many people turn on power-hungry air conditioners. In the middle of a pleasant night in spring or autumn, there is much less demand for electricity. In the early days of electricity, most cities or small regions had their own power utility, which had to meet all of the local demand. The utility needed to have the capacity to supply peak demand, but this meant that it would be running far short of capacity for the rest of the time.

This economically wasteful condition could not be allowed to continue. Today, electric utilities spread around their power, so if a power company in a certain area of the country is having trouble meeting its needs, it can get power from another power company, which is running under capacity. But to do this, power lines from different areas must be interconnected, so that power can be transferred. The power distribution system consists of large, complicated networks called grids.

Although electricity can be efficiently distributed in this way, there is also another, less desirable consequence. A disturbance in one part of the system can affect a widespread area. This is what generally happens during major blackouts.

The blackout in August 2003 apparently began as a loss of power in the northern United States, due in part to losses caused by failure to keep overgrown vegetation away from power lines. In principle, the grid is designed so that power outages stay localized, but since the network is complicated, sometimes there is a cascading effect, and an ever growing number of utilities begin to fail. This is what caused the 2003 blackout, although the details of the event and who, if anyone, was responsible, were not firmly established.

Problems such as these can be reduced by careful planning and by the diligence of grid operators, but they cannot be eliminated. Electricity generation costs money, so everyone must be economical. This means that the complicated networks for electrical power distribution are necessary, and that it is impossible to eliminate errors completely.

But with an increasing population and a continually rising demand, a great strain is put on the world's resources. Sometimes local utilities, stretched beyond capacity and unable to transfer enough power from elsewhere, institute "brownouts." The power continues without interruption, but at a lower voltage, and thus less power, which is the product of voltage and current. This method prevents a blackout, but the lower voltage may cause lights to dim (hence the term *brownout*) and other electrical equipment to malfunction. In other cases, desperate power companies may institute rolling blackouts, whereby the power is shut off to small areas for short periods. The result is a series of miniature blackouts, which roll from one neighborhood to another, as the power company decreases the total demand by taking a portion of their customers offline for a time.

Because the world's power consumption will continue to increase in the future, civilization must develop the ability to expand the world's resources within the constraints imposed by economy and the laws of physics. One way to do that is to find alternative sources of power.

Future Sources of Electrical Power

Electricity is said to be generated, but as noted several times in this book, the physics behind the process involves a transformation. The process converts one form of energy or another into the form of energy we call electricity.

Batteries use the energy from chemical reactions. Electric utility companies typically use electromagnetic induction, which requires work, and therefore energy. The process employed by utility companies transforms whatever energy is used to produce the induction—basically, some form of motion—into the energy of electric charges flowing through circuits.

To drive the motion, utility companies often use steam power. Steam can exert a lot of force and is readily made. As steam does work, it loses some heat and reverts to a liquid state, so it must be reheated periodically. Heat is yet another form of energy, and to produce it requires, by the laws of physics, transforming another source of energy. In the old days, this was usually done by burning wood or coal.

Today, there are many more options. Energy sources for power plants include oil, natural gas, coal, nuclear energy, falling water (from, say, a dam), wind energy and sunlight. Yet with all these options, nearly half of the electrical power generated in the United States during a typical year in the early 21st century is produced by coal. An additional 20 percent is produced from natural gas or oil.

There are several problems with these statistics. One problem is that all of the world's available coal, oil, and gas are being used up. Nature took millions of years to produce these resources, and when they run out, they are gone for good, for people do not have the means to produce more. This problem will continue to get worse, because electricity consumption is increasing. Electricity usage in the United States rose about 25 percent from 1991 to 2002. Given the world's limited resources, this kind of increase is unsustainable without developing alternative sources of energy.

Another problem is that the burning of coal, oil, and gas is not environmentally friendly. Pollution can cause global warming, irreparable damage to the habitats of people and animals, and many other problems, including disorders such as asthma.

These problems are caused in part by society, and in part by the laws of physics, which require the "consumption" of energy—more accurately, a transformation—in order to produce it in a more convenient form. Physicists and other scientists are working on developing alternate sources of energy to fuel the production of electricity. One of the most abundant sources wakes people every day—the Sun. Sunlight is a form of energy, and light is electromagnetic radiation, a special type of propagating electric and magnetic field whose properties are closely associated with but distinct from the electric and magnetic phenomena described in this book. Electricity from solar energy is not only possible but routinely produced.

Yet only a tiny fraction of electrical power in the United States is derived from solar energy. The reason should sound familiar: electricity is difficult to store. Because electricity generally must be consumed as it is produced, solar energy is less than ideal. During noon on days with a clear sky, plenty of sunlight is available; at night, or on cloudy days, there is little or none.

But this need not always be the case. Sunlight never stops: the path is merely blocked on occasion. Rarely is sunlight blocked in space (only during eclipses), and this could be one way of tapping it in a more reliable fashion. Orbiting spacecraft could absorb sunlight and transform it, perhaps, into some other kind of radiation, then beam it down to power production plants. The amount of continuously available sunlight would probably more than make up for the cost of the additional steps of energy transformation required in this process. Light from the Sun can also provide energy to fly *Helios,* an experimental, remotely piloted airplane, flying well above the clouds.

Other feasible approaches include improving the ability to store electricity. As batteries get bigger and better, it may be possible to make more use of the sporadic sunlight that falls on Earth's surface.

Just about any source of energy can be employed to make electricity. One source that engineers and scientists are excited about is called a fuel cell. Fuel cells "burn" hydrogen and produce little if any pollution. At present, fuel cell technology is not fully developed, but once available it may be able to fill a considerable portion of society's electricity needs.

Electricity can even be made from human power. By peddling a rotor—for instance, a rotor driven by the pedals of a bicycle—a person is capable of generating enough electricity to turn on a light

Helios, a solar-powered, remotely piloted aircraft, soars over the Pacific in a 2003 test flight. This kind of aircraft may find use in long-duration flights to monitor weather or provide telecommunication services. *(NASA/Carla Thomas)*

bulb or two. But people power is not likely to solve all the problems. Powering the TV, refrigerator, and air conditioner would require a large family or a lot of friends, and a great deal of sweat.

The laws of physics, at least as they are presently understood, do not encourage a belief that the world's energy problems will be soon fixed with some kind of miraculous invention. There appears to be no such thing as free energy. Electricity most certainly is not free, but there are plenty of energy sources available to convert into electricity. It is vital that present and future physicists learn how to make this transformation efficiently and cleanly if civilization and all of its conveniences and technology are to continue flourishing.

5

MOTION FROM ELECTRICITY

CLIMBING THE 110-FLOOR staircase of the 1,450-foot (442-m) Sears Tower in Chicago would take a lot of effort. Climbing it every morning to go to work would cause even a superbly trained athlete to look for another job. People who work in skyscrapers such as the Sears Tower are fortunate to have another way to get to the office—elevators, driven by electricity.

The electromagnetic research of the physicists Hans Christian Oersted and Michael Faraday, described in the previous chapters, has had many practical applications. A short time after these discoveries Thomas Davenport, a clever self-educated Vermont blacksmith, patented the first electric motor in 1837. Davenport's motor worked, but it was slightly ahead of its time and inefficiency limited its success.

Since that time most of the problems have been overcome, with spectacular results. Motion from electricity is an important part of everyone's life and activities, from taking elevators and riding electric trains to using the electric motors in power drills, garage door openers, car windows, and much else. Newer types of electrical engines also propel space vehicles and may signal the end of the world's reliance on oil and gasoline.

Running on Electricity

Although electricity is common today, motors and motion did not begin with the discovery of electricity. There are other options for performing tasks such as raising and lowering an elevator, and elevators of the early 19th century used steam or high-pressure fluid as an energy source. These early elevators mainly hauled cargo, since people did not trust these machines enough to ride them. Then, in the 1850s, the inventor Elisha Otis developed a feature to prevent an elevator from falling in the case of an accident. Otis's invention was a safety catch that would stop a falling elevator if, in the worst possible case, its cable broke. Soon afterward, elevators for people began to appear in some of the taller buildings.

At the time of the earliest elevators, electric motors were not yet practical for this purpose, but soon electricity replaced all other power sources. Electric elevators proved to be efficient and relatively inexpensive; they also had much more controllable speed, which did not depend on the number of people the elevator was carrying. (Otherwise being on an elevator with a lot of other people meant a long ride up, because the car would not move as quickly.)

One of the simplest features of generating motion from electricity is that it is exactly the opposite of using motion to generate electricity. (According to one story, several people made this discovery when they accidentally hooked up the wires of their electric generator backward!) As described in the sidebar on page 60, electric motors can be thought of as electric generators running in reverse.

Electric motors are found everywhere: in cars (rolling up windows, moving the wiper blades, and doing many other jobs), videocassette recorders (VCRs) and compact disk (CD) players, refrigerators, washer and dryers, garages, and many other places. Almost any small or medium-sized device that has moving parts makes use of some sort of electric motor.

Electric motors have made workers much more productive—jobs that in the past required a lot of time and effort are now done more quickly and easily. Although tightening a bolt may seem too simple to require a motor, the job of tightening thousands of bolts a day is not. Workers in manufacturing plants face these challenges, and turning a wrench by hand many times every day leads to soreness and possible injury. The development of power tools, especially small, portable power tools, greatly increased worker productivity. By the 1920s, small electric motors made big changes

Electric Motors

An electric motor turns electrical energy into motion. The figure shows the main parts of a simple electric motor, which consist of the following parts:

- ◆ A magnet that is sometimes called a field magnet (in small motors this is often a "permanent" magnet)
- ◆ An electromagnet attached to a rotor (which can freely spin)
- ◆ A circuit for sending current through the electromagnet

As discussed in chapter 3, the electromagnet becomes a magnet with a north and a south pole when current flows

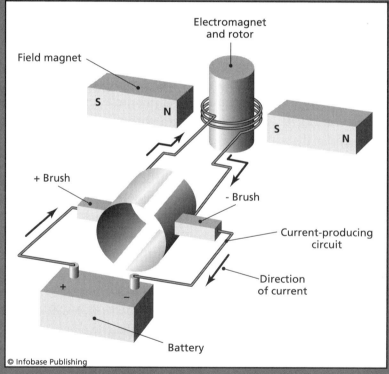

© Infobase Publishing

Alternating current flowing through the electromagnetic rotor periodically reverses its magnetic poles. The magnetism of the field magnet produces a force to spin the electromagnet to align its poles with those of the field magnet (north to south and south to north), but the periodic reversals result in a continual spinning of the rotor.

through the coils. Opposite poles attract, so the electro-magnet's north pole is attracted to the field magnet's south pole, and the electromagnet's south pole is attract-ed to the field magnet's north pole. Because the electro-magnet is on a rotor, the magnetic force will rotate the electromagnet until its poles are aligned to the opposite poles of the field magnet, north to south and south to north.

This attraction generates motion, though only a lit-tle—less than one-half of a complete rotation of the rotor. But suppose that when the electromagnet's poles become aligned with the opposite poles of the field magnet, the current through the electromagnet reverses in direction. In electromagnets, this reversal of current will cause the north and south poles of the magnet to switch. When this happens, the adjacent poles of the electromagnet and field magnet suddenly become alike (the north poles are be-side each other, as are the south poles), and the magnetic force causes the rotor to spin once more so that opposite poles are again aligned. But just as the opposite poles are near each other, the current reverses again, returning to its original direction. Like poles are now aligned and the magnetic force turns the rotor. The process repeats and the rotor continues to spin as long as there is a periodically reversing current flowing through the coils of the electro-magnet.

There are two major types of electric motor, AC and DC. In an AC motor, the current driving the electromagnet is AC. Since AC reverses direction periodically, it is well suited for the job. DC does not reverse direction, so in DC motors, in which DC flows through the electromag-net, some means of reversing the current is necessary. This is often done by making the contacts between the electromagnet and the source of DC slide by each other. The contacts are semicircles, such as the brushes of the DC motor shown in the figure. After each half-spin the connection changes, so the current reverses and keeps the rotor spinning.

Most practical motors are more complicated than this but are based on the same idea. DC motors are easy to build and the spin rate of the rotor is easy to control, but these mo-tors require more maintenance and can be more expensive than AC motors.

This small electric motor opens and closes a garage door. *(Kyle Kirkland)*

in the efficiency of American manufacturing, and these tools were an important part of the innovations that allowed carmakers to make automobiles affordable to the majority of American families.

Today electric motors are used not only to make cars but also to power a lot of their equipment. Power windows and windshield wipers have already been mentioned, and electric motors are important in other ways. For example, modern ignition systems rely on a starter motor. Early gasoline-powered automobiles had to be cranked by hand, usually requiring the driver get out, insert a long pole into a slot near the engine, and rotate it quickly. Inserting a small key from the inside and twisting it are easier and more convenient.

The alternator is another important device in cars. It does not run as a motor, though, since its job is to generate electricity. Power windows and windshield wipers need electrical energy, and although they could get electricity from the car's battery, this would tend to drain the battery rapidly. The alternator provides electricity by using the motion produced by the car's engine. A car's alternator is a good example of an electric motor run in reverse.

Electric Cars and Trains

The engine of almost all cars made in the second half of the 20th century ran on gasoline or diesel fuel. These combustion engines, which burn liquid fuel to transform chemical energy into kinetic energy, emit a large quantity of pollution. Many people began to believe in the 1980s and 1990s that gasoline engines should be avoided and that cars should be powered only by electricity, engine and all. Electric cars, they claimed, were the future. What many of these people did not know was that electric cars were also part of the past.

Car engines in the early 1900s ran on one of three energy sources: electricity, steam, or gasoline. Gasoline engines were extremely loud, unreliable, and smelly. Steam engines took a long time to start on cold mornings and the boiler, which heated water to produce steam, had a dangerous tendency to explode. Electric cars were for a while the most popular type.

But gradually gasoline engines improved, and Henry Ford chose a gasoline engine to power his hugely successful Model T. One of the biggest problems with electric cars was a lack of speed, because batteries could not provide enough energy to generate it. Anyone driving a slow electric car might be advised, rudely, to "get a horse!" Steam and electric cars gradually disappeared.

Although gasoline engines have continued to improve, the pollution they emit has become a problem as the number of cars on the road has increased. The pollution is mostly due to the quickness at which the engines must operate. Complete combustion of gasoline produces only water and carbon dioxide, but car engines operate so quickly that there is not enough time to burn the fuel fully. As a result, other products such as carbon monoxide, hydrocarbons, and nitrogen oxides form and are released into the air, producing the smog that affects big cities such as Los Angeles. Today the number of cars in the world is rapidly approaching a billion, and the problem is getting much worse. And even if gasoline engines completely burned their fuel they might still be creating problems, since carbon dioxide may be contributing to global warming.

Electric cars began to make a comeback in the 1980s, at least on the drawing board. But the same limitation found in the earlier models reappeared. Other difficulties arose as well, including the basic problem, mentioned in earlier chapters, that has always made the physics of electricity troublesome: electricity is hard to store.

Electricity can be stored in batteries until needed, but most batteries cannot store a great quantity of it. Today many car batteries are based on lead-acid, producing electricity from reactions generated by lead *electrodes* dipped in acid. These rechargeable batteries are heavy and bulky but are necessary to power the electric starter and other electric motors while the engine is not running. This kind of battery is useful but alone it cannot supply enough energy to power a car engine. Although batteries are more efficient than gasoline—less energy is wasted as heat—they are not nearly as rich in energy. A gallon of gasoline contains about 60 to 90 times more energy than a lead-acid battery.

Placing a large number of batteries in series is necessary to power the engine of an electric car. If each battery provides 12 volts, 20 batteries in series together produce 240 volts. This is enough to propel a car of average size, although it is not capable of rapid acceleration—merging onto a busy freeway would be a problem. Another problem is that the batteries must be frequently recharged, since about 100 miles of driving depletes them. Although charging the batteries can be as simple as plugging them into a convenient outlet, the process usually takes hours. The batteries are also heavy and expensive and have a limited life.

The great benefit of an electric car is that there are no polluting emissions. Yet this benefit was not enough to convince many car buyers to purchase the electric cars produced in the 1980s and early 1990s, because the cars were expensive and their performance was limited. But since then, newer and better batteries have come along, and a few experimental electric cars have been built that have a range of 300 miles and can accelerate as quickly as the fastest high-performance gasoline-powered cars. One such car is powered by lithium-ion batteries, similar to the batteries that power laptop computers. These cars are not yet practical because they are so expensive, but other electric cars, designed for slow speed instead of highway speed, are economical and are showing up on military bases and college campuses.

The limitations of battery-operated electric cars led engineers to consider adding a small combustion engine to help power the car. This gives the vehicle more power, although it would no longer be a purely electric car with zero emission. This kind of car is a hybrid, powered by both electricity and gasoline. The concept evolved into the *hybrid electric vehicle* (HEV), many of which are on the road today. HEVs made their first appearance on the road in Japan in the late 1990s. A few years later, HEVs began to sell in the United States.

Most HEVs do not need to be plugged in—their gasoline engines are enough to fuel electricity generation. The batteries still have a limited life, but they do not require frequent recharging and

Electric motorcars at Lackland Air Force Base in San Antonio, Texas, help the U.S. Air Force conserve gasoline and yet maintain their mobility around the base. The car's top speed is 25 miles per hour (40 km/hr). *(U.S. Air Force/Raymond V. Whelan)*

so the range of an HEV is the same as that of other cars. With the batteries providing an extra boost, the HEV's gasoline engine can be small. HEVs get good mileage, usually 15–35 miles per gallon (6.3–14.7 km/l) more than purely gasoline-powered cars.

Another big advantage of an HEV is that since batteries supply a portion of the power, it emits fewer pollutants. A powerful engine is necessary only in situations requiring a great deal of force, such as accelerating or climbing a steep hill. At other times, electricity will do the job.

Car manufacturers now offer an increasing number of HEV models to choose from. These cars are slightly more expensive than comparable gasoline-only models, but HEVs are efficient, environmentally friendly, and a good compromise with the difficulties of the physics of electricity.

Purely electric-powered vehicles are more convenient when they do not need batteries but instead rely on electricity generated from an outside source. With cars, providing this source would not be easy because of the excessive amount of wire that would be required to carry electricity to the engine, but this is not an issue for trains running along fixed tracks. Unlike cars, trains powered by electricity are common these days.

The motivation for building electric locomotives appeared early on. Although steam-powered locomotives of the 19th century worked well, riding in a smoke-belching train through a tunnel was an unpleasant, eye-watering experience. When subways began to be built in the latter half of the 19th century, conditions became even worse. One of the first attempts to build an underground railroad in London required the tunnels to be close to the surface so that the exhaust could be vented, but this meant tearing up the streets along the subway's route. Electricity was a clean and efficient alternative, and many railroads, underground or not, began using it. One of the earliest rail lines to go electric in the 1920s and 1930s was a long section of track between New York and Washington, D.C., run by the old Pennsylvania Railroad.

Electric trains get their electricity either from an overhead line or by a rail, often called the third rail, which runs by the side of the train tracks. Power can be DC or AC, but either way the voltage is extremely high and dangerous. Overhead lines using AC are often 25,000 volts, carrying about 10 times less voltage than many utility power lines but still enough to kill a person quickly. Third rails commonly use a smaller but nevertheless hazardous voltage as well, and they are especially dangerous because they are at ground level. In the early days of electric trains, many people unfamiliar with electricity were electrocuted by a third rail because they stepped on one or, in a lapse of both common sense and good hygiene, urinated on one. (Urine is a fair conductor of electricity.)

Trains that get electricity from overhead wires make contact with the wire by a conductor called a pantograph, located on top of the train. The current flows through the train's motor, powering its motion, and then on to ground. In order to make continuous contact with the running train, the overhead wire is supported not only by posts but also by a second wire, sometimes called a messenger wire or catenary. The whole system is maintained by tension to keep the overhead wire straight and steady. If the pantograph loses contact with the overhead wire, then the train loses its power source.

Electric trains operate in many large cities in the United States, including these commuter trains in Philadelphia. *(Kyle Kirkland)*

Since electric trains do not need to store their electricity in batteries, they do not suffer any of the limitations of battery-powered electric cars. Some people hope that electric cars will one day be able to overcome their limitations and become as common as electric trains. But because of the physics of electricity, there is a possibility that HEVs are the best that can be accomplished. Practical, inexpensive cars powered solely by electricity may never be built unless batteries improve (and become more economical) or someone finds a way to deliver electricity conveniently to a moving car.

Electric-powered Craft of the Future

Although improving batteries is not an impossible task, it has problems. One problem is the time required to recharge the batteries. The short range of present-day electric cars is due to the draining of the batteries, which then have to be recharged. But if recharging the batteries only required a short amount of time, then the short range would not be a big concern. Brief refueling stops could be made to extend the journey.

A battery's recharging process transfers electrical energy from the source to the battery, and the transfer proceeds at a rate given by the product of voltage and current. To make the transfer go faster the voltage of the source can be raised—by Ohm's law, this will increase the current (if resistance is kept the same) and allow the recharging equipment to pump electrical energy into the batteries more quickly. But high currents cause a lot of heating, and sometimes gases start to form in the battery. The result is a damaged battery.

Getting around this problem will require creative solutions. One possible solution is to use a large recharging current but only to do so for short periods. By switching a high current on and off repeatedly, electric charge can be transferred quickly and with fewer problems than would be generated by an uninterrupted flow. Although the current would not be present all the time, the overall rate of energy transfer could be increased.

Other promising advances in electric cars could result from more powerful batteries. Lithium batteries, mentioned earlier, are already being tested. These batteries have many advantages, such as high energy density—the battery can store a lot of electricity—and the ability to retain the charges (so that the charges do not "leak" away). But lithium batteries have disadvantages, at least in their present stage of development. Lithium is a dangerous chemical because it is reactive: it will enter into reactions with many other substances and therefore can be difficult to control. Other chemicals used in lithium batteries are flammable, and there is a risk that overheating will produce a fire.

But batteries are the not the only power source possible for future electric-powered craft. All a vehicle needs is to carry around its own electric generator. Diesel-electric locomotives are a good example. Although these trains use diesel fuel, the fuel does not run the motor but instead runs an electric generator. The motor of these locomotives is an efficient electric motor, driven by the output of the generator. Most diesel-fueled trains today are actually diesel-electric.

Trains are big and can carry around heavy generators. A smaller generator would be necessary for vehicles the size and weight of automobiles—yet the generator would still need to supply a lot of power if the automobile were to have capabilities similar to those of cars powered by gasoline engines. A power source for cars that has attracted a lot of attention lately is called a fuel cell. As a battery cell does, a fuel cell produces electricity from chemical reactions. But fuel cells do not rely on reactions in the chemical stored within the cell; fuel cells use some sort of fuel (hence the name), so unlike a battery they do not lose their charge over time. A fuel cell will run as long as its fuel tank is not empty.

Hydrogen fuel cells, which generate electricity from a chemical reaction between hydrogen and oxygen, have often been used to produce electricity in special situations, such as on a spaceship. The hydrogen can be derived from an abundance of substances, such as natural gas or pressurized hydrogen gas, and oxygen can also originate in a number of substances—and if the fuel cell operates in the atmosphere, the oxygen can be from air. Present versions of these fuel cells are expensive, bulky, and not very powerful, so they are not yet ready for a family sedan. Another problem is that, like gasoline, hydrogen is hazardous because it is highly flammable.

If practical hydrogen fuel cells can be developed, they will offer a much cleaner, environmentally friendly source of energy, since the "exhaust" is only heat and some water. Some people think that a practical and inexpensive fuel cell will be developed in just a few years, so they are already talking about a "hydrogen economy"—a means of cheaply producing and distributing a sufficient amount of hydrogen to power most if not all vehicles on the road, in the same way that gasoline today is widely produced and available at filling stations everywhere. If and when a hydrogen economy arrives, society will reap the huge benefits of cleaner air and less dependence on unreliable sources of oil.

Another electric propulsion system in development is the ion engine. Among other applications, this kind of engine promises a significant advance in space travel.

Space-launched rockets use Newton's third law, which says that for every action there is an equal but opposite reaction. Rocket engines emit high-velocity gas molecules out the back end of the vessel (the action) in order to move the rocket forward (the reaction). Conventional rocket engines are chemical and operate by burning a fuel. An ion engine also works by Newton's third law, producing forward thrust by emitting gas, but unlike a chemical engine, which uses a large amount of gas and emits it at a relatively slow speed, an ion engine uses a small amount of gas and emits it at an extremely fast speed. The ion engine therefore uses less fuel. But, in turn, the ion engine needs some means of accelerating the gas. This is where electricity comes into play.

An ion engine works by producing ions, which are atoms or molecules with an electric charge. In one type of ion engine, ions are produced by bombarding a gas with small particles that knock electrons from atoms of the element xenon. This process leaves a small positive charge on the xenon atom—it becomes a positive ion. A voltage accelerates the ions out the back of the engine. As with a conventional rocket, the momentum of the exiting xenon material produces a forward thrust. The difference is that the material is given a boost in speed by electrical means, and this boost in

A xenon ion engine undergoes testing at NASA's Jet Propulsion Laboratory in California. The charged atoms give the engine's emission a faint glow. *(NASA)*

speed increases the thrust of the rocket. (Before the xenon exits the craft, electrons are added back to the atoms; otherwise, the engine would develop an electrical charge from the excess electrons, and this would eventually slow or even stop the engine.)

The National Aeronautics and Space Administration (NASA) used an ion engine in a spacecraft called *Deep Space 1,* launched in 1998. The engine performed so well that NASA extended the mission and the craft went on to visit a comet. Xenon atoms were the propellant, emitted from the engine's nozzle at a speed of about 62,000 miles per hour (100,000 km/hr). The engine did not use much gas and at best it could barely produce a 50th of a pound

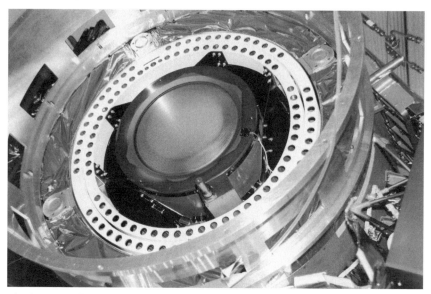

The ion propulsion engine of NASA's *Deep Space 1* probe was the first nonchemical engine to be the main propulsion unit of a spacecraft. *(NASA)*

of thrust—much less than a chemical engine. But the ion engine was far more efficient than a chemical one and made its fuel last. This means that, although slow, the ion rocket got up to speed by running longer.

Ion engines are among the most promising propulsion systems in the future of space exploration. Because the engine cannot accelerate quickly, a conventional chemical engine is generally needed to lift the rocket into space, but ion engines are tens of times more effective than chemical engines over the long haul. Future missions to Mars, and to other planets, may be riding ion engines to their destination.

Motion from electricity provides a lot of opportunities, not just on the surface of the planet but in space as well. Electric motors have vastly improved worker productivity, as well as making everyone's life easier, and vehicles such as electric trains and HEVs have made the world a cleaner, less polluted place. Electricity will also help make the solar system a "smaller" place by powering the ion engines that can span great distances.

6

ELECTRONICS

A N UNDERSTANDING OF the physics of electricity, which resulted from 19th-century science and engineering, completely transformed the world. Electric motors began to supply a convenient source of energy and motion, as described in the previous chapter, and electricity became a necessary utility—cables soon carried electrical power to every home. But electricity went even further. Electric circuits and components became so sophisticated that they could perform billions of calculations per second or help a fighter pilot fly one of the fastest, most maneuverable planes ever built.

Today's world depends on electronics—devices that use electricity. Businesses would collapse without computers, and fighter pilots would be unable to fly. This might seem strange because businesses and planes have not always relied on electronics, and they got along just fine without electricity for a long time.

Electronics is essential today because of speed—and physics. Modern fighter planes are so agile and quick that human pilots cannot respond fast enough to control them. The F-117 Nighthawk Stealth Fighter, for example, is an unstable aircraft. Engineers built instability into the design on purpose because it increased the plane's agility, just as a broomstick balanced on a hand is unstable and therefore moves easily and quickly. But keeping the broomstick balanced is exceptionally difficult,

The F-117 requires sophisticated electronics to help the pilot control the aircraft. *(U.S. Air Force/Staff Sgt. Derrick C. Goode)*

and pilots cannot control a "jumpy" plane without sophisticated electronics.

Several factors were crucial to the development of sophisticated electronic equipment. One factor is physics; another factor is a substance that is the second most abundant element in Earth's crust.

Silicon and Microchips

About 25 percent of the weight of Earth's crust is silicon. But silicon is not found lying around by itself; it exists in nature as part of a compound. Often the compound also contains oxygen, which is the only element in the Earth's crust more common than silicon. After silicon is chemically isolated and in a *crystal* form it looks metallic and has a grayish color. The properties of silicon are so useful in electronics that a part of northern California around San Francisco, which is home to numerous companies involved in electronics and technology, is known as *Silicon Valley*.

Silicon is important in electronics because it can be a *semiconductor*. As discussed in chapter 1, an electrical conductor has a low resistance to the flow of current. The term *semiconductor* might suggest that it has a resistance halfway between those of a conductor and an insulator, but actually semiconductors are more complicated than that. Semiconductors are vital components of circuits mainly because their electrical properties can be altered and controlled.

The physics of semiconductors is complex, but the basic idea involves the movement of charges. Metals are good conductors because some of their electrons are mobile. Electrons in a semiconductor are not nearly as mobile (except under certain conditions, such as when the temperature is high). With the addition of a few extra charges, though, the resistance of the semiconductor can be changed. The extra charges come about by adding a small amount of another substance to the semiconductor; these substances are sometimes called impurities because they are added in such tiny amounts (only about one atom per million of the semiconductor). The process is known by the unappealing term *doping*.

The addition of mobile charges can change a semiconductor into a conductor. A good analogy is what happens to water when salt is added. Pure water is a poor conductor, but salt dissolves into ions that are mobile and can carry electricity, so salty water is an effective conductor. Water can even be tested for the presence of impurities by how well it conducts electricity—tap water in most cities conducts a small but noticeable amount of electricity.

Semiconductors with impurities that provide extra electrons are called n-type semiconductors. Another type of semiconductor, the p-type, has extra places into which electrons can move. These places are called holes, and physicists often think of them as positive charges (opposite to those of the negatively charged electron). The real business of electronics starts when p- and n-type semiconductors are placed beside each other. A p-n junction, for example, forms by adding the appropriate impurities to adjacent areas of a semiconductor. These junctions are the basis for an enormously wide range of electronics today.

A p-n junction is useful because if a small positive voltage is applied to the p-type side, the negative electrons of the n-type side have an electrical force pushing them across the junction, and a current flows. But if a negative voltage is applied to the p-type side, the opposite situation occurs and no current flows. The voltage is called a bias voltage and it controls the flow of current across the junction. Current only flows one way and a p-n junction forms a diode, which is a one-way valve for electricity that can be open or closed. Two junctions together is either a p-n-p or an n-p-n region and is called a *transistor*. The sidebar further explores diodes and transistors.

Diodes and Transistors

The earlier sidebar on Ohm's law contained a plot of voltage as a function of current. The plot was a straight line. A diode behaves slightly differently, as shown in the figure. Note that this diagram is a plot of current (vertical axis) versus voltage (horizontal axis), and the slope of the curve represents conductance, the inverse of resistance. This diode conducts—has a low resistance—only the right side of the diagram. On the left side of the diagram (where the voltage is negative) the resistance is large, so even high voltages produce only a small amount of current, as seen in the relatively flat curve. The current-voltage curve shows that a diode will conduct only when the applied voltage exceeds the small amount necessary to push charges across the semiconductor. When the voltage is lower, or has the opposite sign (negative in the case of this diode), little current flows.

One of the first uses of diodes was in radio receivers. Diodes performed rectification—the current of the received signal, which could flow in either direction, was forced to go in only one direction. Rectification was part of the process that retrieved the information carried by the radio wave.

Diodes are useful in a huge number of other ways. A *light-emitting diode* (LED) is a particularly common example. Electrons moving across the p-n junction give off electromagnetic radiation, but usually this radiation is not of the right frequency to be visible or it is blocked or absorbed by the material. But with the right configuration, the radiation becomes visible light and the diode becomes an LED. LEDs are frequently used as indicators, such as the little light on a computer that shows it has power.

The first diodes were quite different from today's diodes. Early diodes were vacuum tubes that looked somewhat like light bulbs. Vacuum tubes contain a filament (a thin wire) that emits electrons when heated. A charged plate in the vacuum tube attracts the electrons so that they can only flow one way, making the vacuum tube behave as a diode does. But all modern electronic components are made from semiconductor p-n junctions because of their advantages over the old vacuum tubes: reliability, smaller size,

Transistors are even more useful. John Bardeen, Walter Brattain, and William Shockley invented the transistor in 1947 at Bell Telephone Laboratories in Murray Hill, New Jersey, and they were awarded the 1956 Nobel Prize in physics for their work. A transistor has three terminals, each belonging to one of the "doped" regions of the p-n-p or n-p-n junctions. A potential or current on one junction affects the conductivity of the other, much as a diode does but offering more control possibilities. Transistors behave as valves that can open to a varying extent and allow a varying amount of current through them. They are often used as fast electrical on-off switches, where they control the flow of current in equipment such as the computational circuitry of computers.

Transistors are also useful in amplifying weak signals, and one of the first important applications of the transistor was in hearing aids. A transistor is excellent for this purpose because it boosts audio signals (after the device transforms the signals into electric current) and is small enough to fit into a small space. The hearing aid converts the amplified signal back into sound, which is then loud enough to be heard by the wearer.

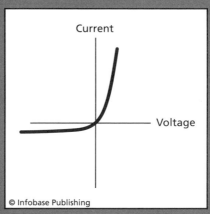

© Infobase Publishing

The current–voltage relation for a diode is a tale of two curves. For the diode represented by this curve, only positive voltages (the right side of the diagram) can produce a current in the diode. The steeply rising part of the curve signifies a high conductance (low resistance), while the flat part of the curve indicates a low conductance (high resistance).

and less heat. The Electronic Numerical Integrator and Computer (ENIAC), one of the first electronic computers ever built, in 1946 at the University of Pennsylvania, used vacuum tubes and was so large it filled an entire room, which had to be cooled by industrial-strength fans. Although ENIAC was the marvel of its day, today's 10-dollar pocket calculators are faster and more powerful.

Despite their enormous advantages, silicon semiconductors are not easy to make. Because their electrical properties can be altered by the presence of even small amounts of impurities, semiconductors must be manufactured in exceptionally clean (and expensive) rooms. The semiconductor material is also critical. Early semiconductors were made of the element germanium. Although this element continues to be used for some applications, the most common material these days is silicon, thanks to its low cost and relative ease of handling and processing compared to other elements.

Semiconductor junctions, and transistors in particular, rank among the most useful inventions in history. Yet even further advances occured when transistors and other semiconductor components were miniaturized. Instead of making a circuit consisting of fingernail-sized transistors, people began to make all of the components on a small, thin wafer of silicon—a microchip (or just "chip") of silicon. This is the *integrated circuit* (IC), named because all of the circuit elements are integrated into a single chip.

Although electronics had begun to shrink because of the introduction of transistors, the silicon IC chip reduced the size even more impressively. Devices that once required entire rooms, such as ENIAC, could fit into a small box the size of a loaf of bread. Jack Kilby made the first IC in 1959 while working at a company called Texas Instruments. The earliest ICs contained small circuits with only a few transistors but were crucial in such important projects as the Apollo moon landings. Modern ICs are made with "very large-scale integration" (VLSI) and contain millions of transistors, all within an area the size of a paper clip.

An individual chip may be inexpensive, but the initial setup and design are not. Engineering a chip design with millions of circuit elements is not easy, and manufacturers must spend large sums of money to buy and maintain clean rooms and the complex equipment needed to build and test the chips. But once the design is finished and the manufacturing process is in place, highly useful chips can be made by the batch. ICs are vital components of microwave ovens, cell phones, cars, and much else, and they have transformed society as nothing else has in the last few decades.

Fighter planes would also be lost without IC chips—as would their pilots. This was true even as far back as the 1970s, when the F-14 Tomcat fighter became operational. Instead of slower electromechanical systems, the plane used chip-based computers because they were smaller and more reliable. Today the most advanced planes are "fly-by-wire": they are so fast and maneuverable that electronic equipment is essential. Electronics is also used in big planes such as jetliners in order to increase the safety of their operation.

ICs are also essential components of all modern computers. They perform a number of different jobs, not the least of which are computational processes, performed by the computer's *central processing unit* (CPU). The computer's IC is so small it is called a microprocessor, and though its size has remained small, the number of transistors has grown to an amazing number. One of the first microprocessors was the 4004, made by a company called Intel and introduced in 1971. It contained 2,250 transistors. Intel's Itanium 2 processor, introduced in 2003, contains 410,000,000 transistors.

Computers

Computers changed the world as much as any other development in the 20th century. Before the invention of ICs, computer CPUs were made from hundreds or thousands of separate components, either transistors or vacuum tubes or, even earlier, moving parts such as gears or levers. ICs reduced the size of computers from room-occupying monsters to a box that fits on a small desk. The bulk of most home computers today comes from accessories and wiring, not the parts that do the computation. The heart of the computer is a tiny microprocessor.

A computer consists of a CPU, memory, and a number of input and output devices by which data are entered or displayed. The components are connected by wires in which small electric currents flow, and the main connections are made through a path known as the bus. The operations occur in precise time sequences governed by a timer or clock. The computer carries out instructions in machine language, which is binary—there are only two "letters," 0 and 1. Binary language is tiresome for humans—as is the sequence of operations a computer must go through to do even one calculation—but it enormously simplifies the computer's circuitry. Programming a computer to carry out a set of instructions using only binary language would be a time-consuming task, but fortunately people can program computers today by using various "high-level" programming languages such as BASIC and C. Programs called compilers or interpreters, already written and installed on the machine, translate these human-understandable programs into the appropriate binary language instructions.

Contrary to popular belief, computers are not capable of carrying out complicated instructions. Computers are simple machines. At each tick of the clock the computer acts on a basic instruction (or a set of basic instructions) and processes some amount of data obtained from its memory unit. It repeats this procedure as often as necessary to finish its assigned tasks. The utility of computers lies not in their ability to implement complex instructions but their ability to implement simple ones quickly. A sequence of simple instructions can accomplish a complicated task if the program and the data are correct.

The speed and power of computers have been increasing rapidly in recent years. The increase in the number of transistors per microprocessor, as described in the previous section, gave rise to Moore's law, named after Gordon Moore (one of the founders of Intel). Moore's law says that the capacity of computers doubles every 18–24 months. Over the last few decades this "law" has held true, although some people wonder how long the trend can continue. Moore's law cannot continue to be accurate indefinitely because it will eventually encounter other, more powerful laws—the laws of physics—that tend to be restrictive. Some of these laws involve quantum mechanics, the branch of physics governing the motion of small particles. In order to put an ever-growing number of components on a small chip, the size of each component must decrease, and eventually this reduction would lead to particles small enough to be affected by quantum mechanics. Such particles are difficult or impossible to control, putting a limit on any further size reduction of electronic computers.

Important factors in the performance of the small computers used in homes and businesses include clock speed and the size and type of *random access memory* (RAM). The clock speed is given in hertz, a unit of cycles per second. In 2005 the fastest inexpensive desktop computers operated at around 3 gigahertz, or 3 billion cycles per second. In general, the faster the clock runs, the faster the computer can work. RAM holds the programs and data on which the computer is operating, and since many programs (especially video games) are large, having a lot of RAM is necessary. Without enough RAM the computer must place some of its data on the hard disk, an event that slows the operation down to a crawl, since it is much slower to store and retrieve data on the hard disk than to do so using RAM.

Governments, corporations, and especially scientists and engineers need faster, more expensive computers. These computers often have more than one CPU, along with huge amounts of memory, and execute many programs at the same time. *Supercomputer* is the term used to describe the fastest computers, but because of how rapidly computers evolve, the term is relative: a small home computer today is as fast as the best supercomputer available 20 years ago.

Computer engineers measure the performance of supercomputers in *floating point operations per second* (FLOPS). Like the clock speed of small computers, FLOPS is not a perfect measurement of performance, but it is a good overall indicator. The fastest single supercomputer in 2005 could perform over 280,000,000,000,000 FLOPS. This speed record will only hold for a short time—even faster computers will soon be available—but it is amazingly fast. For comparison, most people are capable of only about 0.01 FLOPS or even less.

Supercomputers today can do in a reasonable time computations that would previously have taken years or decades. Weather forecasting, models of global warming, engineering design, and scientific research are examples. Computers have become indispensable in physics laboratories, and high-performance computers are also heavily used in industry, particularly in computer-aided design (CAD). Most of today's technology is so complex that devices would be impossible or prohibitively expensive to design without CAD programs. Consider trying to design by hand Intel's Itanium 2 processor with its 410,000,000 transistors. Manufacturers can use computer programs to test a new type of automobile or aircraft without actually building the vehicle, saving a huge amount of time and money.

Other computer applications include virtual reality, in which the interaction between human and computer is richer and more human-oriented than it is with a simple keyboard, mouse, and monitor. Most computers get their input from a human operating the keyboard or mouse. The computer performs some sort of calculation and displays the result for the human operator on a screen or monitor. Virtual reality immerses the human operator in an environment that has more of a real-world feel. For instance, the physics of molecular forces can be simulated such that the human

Advances in electronics and computers allow the lifelike simulation of many situations, including aerial combat. *(U.S. Air Force/1st Lt. Nathan D. Broshear)*

operator actually experiences the forces through special devices attached to his or her hands and head. These simulations inspire a better understanding than a simple two-dimensional picture on a monitor because they appeal to more senses, or at least to a more appropriate sense for a particular application. The simulation seems more real and more vivid.

Even though computer applications are becoming more sophisticated, computers are still just machines. They do not think: they merely perform a sequence of simple instructions very quickly. Computer scientists believe there are problems so difficult that they cannot possibly be solved by computers, no matter how fast computers ever become. But that does not stop scientists from trying to develop "smarter" computers.

Artificial intelligence involves computers or computer-like objects that attempt to solve problems as a human would, by applying reasoning from analogy or experience. Physics offers an important example—a small number of laws can be applied to solve a large number of problems—and this is how humans generalize knowledge and simplify problems. Researchers have been working

Smart robots may one day aid astronauts in exploring the surfaces of other worlds, if scientists can learn how to mimic human intelligence with a computer. *(NASA)*

on artificial intelligence for decades, but progress has been slow. Getting a computer to do a simple task quickly and repetitively is easy compared to getting one to generalize or simplify. Because scientists do not fully understand the details of how people think, it has been extremely difficult to design a computer to replicate the process.

One application of computers that has not been slow in development is the global computer network known as the Internet. This network ties together computers all over the world and underlies the World Wide Web, email, and much else. A vast amount of information is available on Web sites: from just a few Web "pages" in the 1990s, the Web has grown to an estimated hundreds of billions of documents today. The information is so enormous that "search engines" are essential in order to find specific items, and in 2005 the Internet search engine Google claimed to index over 8 billion Web pages. The Internet is such a busy place because so many people use it, as shown in a 2003 survey by the United States Department of Commerce, which found over half of households in the country have Internet connections. This survey indicated that the Internet has even become important for business as well, since more than half of the people who use the Internet buy goods and services via Web sites, and a quarter of people are banking online.

Tuning In—Radio Tuners

Although the Internet is popular, a much older means of transmitting information still exists today in radio, which has been around for more than 100 years. Almost every home in the 1930s and 1940s had a radio; it was the basis for much of a family's home entertainment until television arrived. The physics of radio is particularly interesting because it involves a number of different branches of physics, including electromagnetic radiation and a phenomenon called *resonance* as well as electronics. The radio receiver, or tuner, continues to be important today, not only because radio and television transmissions are important but also because wireless technology such as cell phones and wireless networks uses the same ideas.

Radio waves form only a small part of the electromagnetic radiation *spectrum*—its range of frequencies. Scientists classify radiation in terms of its frequency, and radio waves are radiation with a frequency of less than a few gigahertz (billion hertz). Radio waves are the lowest frequency on the electromagnetic spectrum, far below the frequency of visible light. Transmission of radio waves uses amplifiers to boost the signal and antennas to radiate the energy into space—in other words, to broadcast. Reception is a problem since the space around a city or neighborhood is filled with a huge number of radio waves of various frequencies, from tens of hertz up to a gigahertz. Finding the right channel in all of that noise is a process of selection—and physics.

A radio receiver tunes into the right channel on the basis of the channel's frequency. Radiation of all different frequencies hits the antenna, but the tuner passes one frequency (actually a small band of frequencies) and rejects the rest. The tuner is an electric circuit employing two special components, a capacitor and an inductor. The sidebar on page 86 describes the electrical properties of *capacitance* and *inductance*.

The capacitance and inductance in a radio circuit select a specific frequency because of resonance. All objects have a resonant (or "natural") frequency with which they vibrate most easily. When an object is struck with some sort of stimulus that comes and goes at the same frequency as the object's resonant frequency, the object will oscillate much more strongly than when struck at any other frequency. Electric circuits do something similar, and the *natural frequency* of electric circuits is given by the capacitance and inductance. Input signals whose frequency is at the resonant frequency can pass through the circuit, but signals at other frequencies cannot.

When the information in the radio wave is recovered, amplified, and sent to a speaker, the radio receiver has done its job. The height or amplitude of the radio wave contains the information in amplitude modulation (AM), which is commonly used for frequencies around 500 to 1,600 kilohertz (thousand hertz). Frequency variations around a fixed carrier frequency contain the information in frequency modulation (FM), and FM stations are found

Capacitance and Inductance

All electric circuits have some amount of capacitance and inductance, but it is often necessary to insert a specific amount of capacitance or inductance into a circuit. This is accomplished by using components called capacitors and inductors.

Capacitance is due to the separation of electric charges. If a voltage source such as a battery acts on two conductors that are close together but not touching, charges will accumulate on the conductors. The charges move because of the potential difference (the voltage), but unlike a complete circuit, they cannot flow across the space between the conductors unless the voltage is exceptionally high. Because of the relationships described by Coulomb's law, charges of opposite sign collect on the separated conductors. This process continues until the charges on the conductors create a potential difference equal to that of the battery, at which time no more charges move and the capacitor is "charged." The amount of capacitance C is given by a simple formula in terms of Q, the amount of charge, and V, the voltage:

$$C = Q/V$$

Capacitors are usually made by placing two small conducting plates in close proximity, as shown in the figure.

Inductance works much differently, but as a capacitor does, an inductor stores energy. A capacitor stores energy in the separation of charges (existing across the two separated conductors), which can produce a current through a conductor. An inductor is a coil and produces a current by electromagnetic induction. As described in chapter 3, electric currents generate magnetic fields, and an inductor takes advantage of this process. Current flowing through the inductor's coil creates a magnetic field, which stores energy because when the current is turned off the magnetic field changes—it gradually falls to zero—and the change produces a current (this is the basis of electromagnetic induction, hence the name *inductor*). The current flows briefly in the direction opposite to the original current. The inductance L of a coil is given by

$$L = N\varphi/I$$

where N is the number of turns of the coil, φ is the strength of the magnetic field through the coil, and I is the current.

A circuit containing both a capacitor and an inductor has a useful property. An example of such a circuit is shown in the figure. Suppose the capacitor is initially charged (by a battery, perhaps) and then someone connects it to an inductor. The charges will flow through the inductor as the capacitor discharges its energy. This current lasts a short time because the capacitor quickly exhausts its charges, and unlike a battery, it cannot separate charge itself (and so it cannot produce a steady current). But as the current fades, the inductor's changing magnetic field produces a current in the opposite direction. This current charges the capacitor again, though in the opposite direction. Once the inductor's energy is spent, the capacitor discharges again. The cycle repeats as long as the capacitor and inductor are connected, and the circuit oscillates as the current goes back and forth. (It will eventually stop in this circuit because the resistance of the wire introduces losses.) The oscillation has a frequency determined by the capacitance and inductance in the circuit.

When connected, a charged capacitor and an inductor produce an oscillation, as the current flows back and forth, charging and discharging the capacitor.

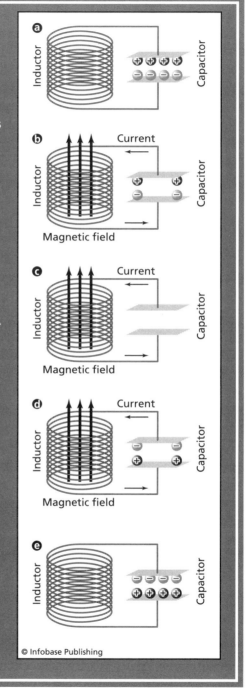

between 85 and 110 megahertz (million hertz). Radio tuners select the station by its frequency, often given by the radio announcer, as in "This is 101.5 on your FM dial" (the frequency in this case is 101.5 megahertz). Turning the dial will change stations because the dial changes either the capacitance or the inductance of the resonant circuit.

Radio wave transmission and reception are used not only by radio stations and receivers. Cell phones and cordless phones, television, satellite communications, wireless networks, and many other applications use radio waves or radiation of a similar frequency. But all of these applications are occurring at the same time and, in many instances, in the same place. This presents a problem known in physics as interference. Tuners select the channel by its frequency, but any other transmission using this frequency will be selected and amplified as well, even if the signal is not desired. Noise appears, sometimes strongly enough to override the desired signal.

High-powered transmissions, called broadcasts, intended to reach a wide audience usually require a government license. Licenses and regulation are necessary so that transmissions do not interfere. But interference is becoming an increasing problem as cell phones and wireless networks grow more popular. Even computer peripherals such as keyboards and mice can communicate with wireless technology, the advantages of which are freedom of movement and elimination of the need for troublesome cables.

But with all this transmission, space is full of radio waves. The government imposes minimal regulation on wireless standards such as Bluetooth and Wi-Fi (Wireless Fidelity) that use low power because they are not broadcasting—they only reach a short range. But this also means the connection can sometimes be shaky because of the low power and the occasional presence of other devices that cause interference. Although wireless technology continues to expand, people must be careful so that the world is not consumed in a babble of competing voices.

Seeing from a Distance: Television

The ease and mobility of wireless communication mean that the number of applications will keep growing. Television, one of the most popular forms of home entertainment, has also grown and evolved recently. These changes do not just involve the way television signals are transmitted but also the way that the electronics of television work.

Television sets in earlier times always consisted of a *cathode ray tube* (CRT). A CRT uses a beam of negatively charged electrons (emitted from a device called a cathode) that are accelerated by electric forces (Coulomb's law). The electron beam must be operated in a vacuum because electrons are so small that air molecules disrupt the beam, so the chamber or tube is an enclosed space with virtually all of the air pumped out. The beam emerges from the rear of the tube and strikes the front face; this face contains a coat of phosphor, which emits light when a high-energy beam of electrons strikes it. The signals received by the television's tuner magnetically control the beam's flight, and the television forms a series of pictures on the phosphor screen. The pictures come and go in a thirtieth of a second, so quickly that the human eye and brain cannot distinguish individual pictures and instead perceive a moving picture.

CRT technology owes a lot to physics. Physicists played an important role in the development of CRTs because these devices were among the first particle accelerators. In the early 1900s, physicists used CRTs to study the properties of tiny particles whose presence could only be detected by such events as seeing the light from a phosphor screen.

The forces required to accelerate electron beams to high speed require large electric fields. In terms of electronics, this means high voltage is necessary, making CRT-based television sets dangerous. These televisions also use a lot of capacitors, which as mentioned earlier store energy in the form of separated electric charges. Capacitors become charged to high voltages during the operation of the television, and sometimes they will hold their charge for a period after the set is turned off. A capacitor will discharge if there is an available path, but in some circuits there are no conductors to allow this to happen. Even in an unplugged CRT television there could be charged capacitors waiting for an opportunity to discharge, and this could occur through the body of an inquisitive person who reaches inside.

CRTs are cheap and work well, so television manufacturers still use them. Video displays such as computer monitors also use CRTs. But other options that offer advantages over this old technology are also available.

A *liquid crystal display* (LCD) is thin, flat, and much lighter in weight than the bulky CRTs. LCDs are useful for computer monitors as well as small displays on watches or cell phones. The physics of the working material is peculiar because it has properties of both liquids and crystals—a crystal is normally a solid with a specific geometrical structure, which is quite different from a flowing liquid!

The liquid crystals used in LCDs have optical properties that are affected by electric fields, but these molecules do not emit light, unlike the phosphor screen of a CRT, so an LCD must get its light from another source. This source in some LCDs is fluorescent tubes arranged in the display. Electric fields affect the passage of this light through the layers of liquid crystals because the electric fields change the properties of these crystals. The screen of an LCD television or monitor consists of a lot of small pixels whose brightness and color are governed by electric signals, such as from a television tuner or cable. Together the pixels form an image. In one type of LCD, a matrix of transistors maintains the electrical state of the pixels so that the display is clearer.

Plasma televisions, like LCDs, are very thin. Plasma televisions get their name from their use of a plasma, which is a gas containing charged particles called ions. The display consists of thousands of tiny cells that contain a plasma (usually a mixture of ionized neon and xenon) trapped between plates of a transparent material such as glass. A current through the cell causes the ions to move, stimulating the emission of electromagnetic radiation. The frequency of this radiation is not in the visible range, but when it strikes a phosphor material in the display, the phosphor emits visible light. The picture appears because electrical signals control the activity of the cells, forming an image. Plasma televisions can support screens of a huge size and offer a bright display with good contrast. Their major disadvantages are that they use a lot of power and are currently expensive.

Physicists and engineers are working on other materials whose electrical properties may also be suitable for video displays. One promising group of materials is the organic light-emitting diode (OLED), which is made of large organic (carbon-containing) molecules that form a semiconductor. OLEDs emit light similarly to LEDs but can make a display when they are deposited in an array on a surface. These displays can be incredibly thin, and because OLEDs emit light they do not need an external source of light, unlike LCDs. OLED displays are so thin they can "printed" onto a flexible material such as a piece of cloth or paper. At the present state of technology these displays are not durable and do not last long, but future research will probably change that. Wearable televisions, or perhaps a mobile one that can be folded and stored in a pocket, may be available within the next five or 10 years.

Superconductors

All the circuits previously discussed in this section use conductors in one form or another to provide a path for electric charges to travel. Most conductors are metal, such as copper wire or a tiny amount of metal deposited on an IC. Although these conductors are effective, they are not perfect because they have at least a small amount of resistance, which means some of the current is wasted. But this is not true of a special type of conductor discovered in 1911 by the Dutch physicist Heike Kamerlingh Onnes (1853–1926).

Onnes was working with materials that had been cooled to extremely low temperatures. He reasoned that the resistance of a conductor at a low temperature would be less than at room temperature because there would be less vibration in the atoms and molecules—all atoms and molecules are in motion, even in a solid material, and the amount of this motion depends on temperature. But Onnes unexpectedly discovered that at the frigid temperature of −451.8°F (−268.8°C), the mercury he was working with (which was a solid at that temperature) suddenly lost all of its resistance! At this temperature it became a *superconductor*—there was no resistance to the flow of charges. Onnes won the Nobel Prize in physics in 1913 for this discovery.

Since a superconductor has no resistance, once a current is set into motion it will flow forever. No one can watch a superconductor long enough to make sure, but currents do last for years and show no sign of losing strength. Superconductors are extremely useful materials because none of the energy of the moving charges is lost.

In an ideal world, all circuits would be made with superconductors. This goal is not yet attainable because while many substances display the property of superconductivity, they do so only at exceptionally low temperatures. Above a certain temperature they are normal, resistance-bearing conductors, and below that temperature (called the critical temperature) they are superconductors. Cooling a substance is more expensive than the loss of energy due to the resistance of room-temperature conductors, so it is not yet economical to use superconductors for everyday tasks.

But this might change in the future. In the 1980s, people began to discover certain types of materials called ceramics that are superconductors at higher temperatures. Recent materials have achieved superconduction at temperatures as high as −211°F (−135°C). Although not exactly warm—and a good distance from a room temperature of 72°F (22°C)—this is a step in the right direction.

The process of discovering higher-temperature superconductors would be easier if the physics of superconduction were better understood. In 1957 the American physicists John Bardeen (1908–91), Leon Cooper (1930–), and J. Robert Schrieffer (1931–) proposed the presently accepted theory, which is known as the BCS theory, named after the last initials of the scientists. The physics is complex and involves quantum mechanics. One of the main ideas is that the electrons moving in a superconductor pair up and weave their way through the material's structure on a special type of wave. The physicists received the 1972 Nobel Prize in physics for their contribution. (It was the second such prize for John Bardeen, who had won earlier for his work on semiconductors and transistors.)

But the BCS theory does not tell the whole story, and it seems to apply only to materials that become superconductors at −387°F (−233°C) or below. The ceramic substances mentioned earlier apparently obey other rules. In the absence of a satisfactory overall theory, the research on superconductors must be trial and error: do something and see whether it works, and if it does not, do something else. Discoveries are slower by this method, if they occur at all. Physicists continue to search for materials that become superconductors at ever higher temperatures, but no one knows how high the temperatures can go. Scientists such as David Larbalestier, at the University of Wisconsin's Applied Superconductivity Center, study the structure of both low- and high-temperature superconductors in hopes of discovering the fundamental principles and how best to apply them to practical situations.

If physicists ever do discover a room-temperature superconductor, this would have profound effects in electronics. Superconductors have already found plenty of applications, even though they must be cooled in order to work. Superconductors are useful in making powerful electromagnets, many of which can be found in the MRI machines mentioned in chapter 2 as well as the huge particle accelerators of today.

Superconductors are also important in a device known as a superconducting quantum interference device (SQUID). SQUIDs are sensitive detectors of magnetic fields and are so effective that they can even detect the tiny magnetic field of a person's head. This field exists because brain cells produce small electric currents, and these currents generate magnetic fields, as governed by the laws of physics that describe all such electromagnetic effects, whether in a copper wire or a brain cell. The measurement of these small magnetic fields, called magnetoencephalography, is another way for scientists to study the activity of the human brain without having to open up the skull, as discussed in more detail in chapter 8. Most of these applications use the lower-temperature superconductors, as the relatively high-temperature ceramics have not yet found a lot of applications because the material is brittle and their superconductive properties are less stable.

Materials that become superconductors at room temperatures or higher would allow many more applications. For instance, the electronic equipment discussed in this chapter could be made smaller and much more efficient. Power companies could transport electricity with no losses, a great economic benefit that would reduce everyone's electric bill. Although electronics has already achieved much—computers, control of fast jet planes, radio and television—there is still more that the physics of electricity can help accomplish.

7

RECORDING AND STORING MUSIC AND MOVIES

ALMOST EVERYONE ENJOYS at least some type of music. But prior to the 20th century, people who wanted to hear music had only two choices: they could make the music themselves or they could go to a concert hall and listen to a live performance. In the 19th century, live music was extremely popular and concerts—where orchestras played music that today would be called classical—had large audiences. Operas were also popular, although in those days many of them were comedies with simple themes and numerous pranks and jokes.

As physicists began to understand the principles of electromagnetism, as discussed in the previous chapters of this volume, engineers and technicians used this new knowledge to develop a third option for music lovers—listening to music from a machine. Because of music's popularity, recording and storing music were among the earliest applications of electricity and magnetism. Later, the physics of electromagnetism became important in recording and storing movies as well as music.

Music from a Machine

In 1877, Thomas Edison invented one of the earliest machines to store and reproduce human speech. The machine was called a phonograph (from the Greek words for sound and writing), and it recorded sound as little hills or valleys on the surface of a cylinder, which was covered by a material such as tin foil or wax.

Sound consists of waves—variations in air pressure that the human ear detects because the waves cause the eardrum to vibrate. Edison focused the sound waves on a sharp instrument that vibrated, somewhat as an eardrum does, against the surface of the cylinder as it spun on its axis. These vibrations made impressions on the surface that could be replayed and turned into sound again. Speech, singing, or music could be captured and stored for later use.

Flat disks, which became known as records, soon replaced cylinders. Records stored sound wave signals in a small groove that spiraled around the disk. Instead of the hills and valleys of a cylinder, small bumps in the walls of the groove represented pressure waves. Many of these records in the 20th century were made of polyvinyl chloride (PVC), and became known as vinyl records. (PVC, a type of hard plastic, is commonly used today to make pipes.)

The earliest record players were mechanical, but the sound quality was poor. (Another problem was that the record had to be turned by hand, so listening to a favorite song over and over again resulted in a sore arm.) But then came electromagnetism, and the situation vastly improved.

After the development of electromagnetic methods, record players used a moving magnet or a moving coil. The magnet or coil responded to the bumps in the record's groove because these variations caused a small movement that produced an electric current by electromagnetic induction. If the record player used a moving magnet, the small movements induced a current in a nearby coil; if the record player used a moving coil, it was placed in a magnetic field so that its motion would induce a current. Either way, the record player employed electromagnetism to translate the small movements, caused by the bumps on the record, into a corresponding electrical signal. Variations in the electrical signal—for example, variations in the strength of the current—corresponded to air pressure waves of the original sound. The machine amplified the signals (because they were usually small) and sent them to a speaker, which turned the electrical signals into sound waves.

Spectral Analysis and the Fourier Transform

Jean Baptiste Joseph Fourier (1768–1830), a French mathematician, made an astonishing discovery that most other mathematicians refused to believe at first. Fourier claimed that any periodic function—such as a wave that repeats itself over time—was made of a sum of other, simpler waves called sine and cosine waves. If the wave is a sound wave, the sine and cosine waves represent "pure" tones or single frequencies. This means that any sound, no matter how complex, can be thought of as being composed of a group of pure tones added together.

Fourier was correct, and his discovery is the basis of spectral analysis. One way of looking at spectral analysis is to consider two different representations of a wave. A wave can be drawn

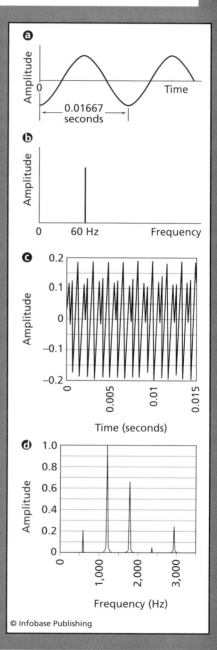

This figure shows two examples of spectral analysis. A 60-hertz sine wave, shown as a plot of amplitude over time in a (the time domain), has a simple frequency domain representation, shown in b. A more complicated wave, whose time domain can be seen in c, has multiple frequency components, as shown by its frequency domain representation, d.

© Infobase Publishing

as a plot that shows the *amplitude* or strength of the wave as it varies over time. This is called the time domain. Part a of the figure shows a simple example of a time domain plot, a graph of a 60-hertz sine wave.

A wave can also be studied by breaking it down into its component frequencies—its spectrum. This is the frequency domain, as shown in part b of the figure. Part b is a graph of the spectral analysis of the sine wave whose time domain appears in part a. This is a particularly simple example, since a pure sine wave has only a single frequency (60 hertz in this case). What Fourier showed was that the two representations were equivalent. The wave is the same; the only thing that is different is the way it is drawn and analyzed. Fourier even supplied the mathematical technique, called the Fourier transform, to go back and forth between the time and frequency domains.

The second half of the figure illustrates a more complicated example. Part c is the time domain representation of a wave and d shows the frequency domain representation. From d it is obvious that the wave has several frequency components of varying magnitude.

Spectral analysis and Fourier transforms have a tremendous number of applications in just about every field of science and engineering. Earthquake analysis is particularly important, for such events are difficult to study and scientists need to squeeze every bit of knowledge from the available data. The improvement of sensors to measure earthquake waves has meant an increase in high-quality data, and when scientists can match certain earthquake frequencies with specific types of geological activity, it will become easier to predict earthquakes.

Biologists also use frequency analysis to study signals recorded from various structures and organs of living organisms. For instance, the electrical activity of the brain, as described in the following chapter, exhibits frequency differences at certain times and in certain regions. Although no one is certain what these frequency differences mean, they offer clues to help scientists understand this enormously complex biological system.

Despite the improvements, the sound heard on even the most expensive of the early record players did not sound natural. The round-trip from sound to vinyl record and back again changed some of the sound's characteristics, and the difference was notice-able—music or speech sounded scratchy or tinny. One of the most important characteristics of sound is its frequency content. As described in the sidebar on page 96, spectral analysis is the process of examining a wave or oscillation in terms of its spectrum.

One of the reasons early music-making machines did not repro-duce sound well is that they failed to reproduce all of the original sound's frequencies. Speech or music reproductions do not sound the same as the original when some of the original frequency content is missing or has changed in relative strength. The result is a distor-

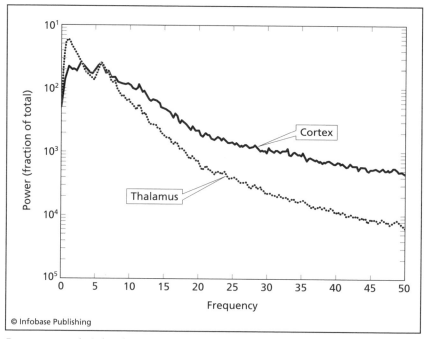

Frequency analysis has been used here to study the frequencies of brain waves recorded electrically from two different parts of a mouse's brain. The horizontal axis specifies the frequency, while the vertical axis is a measure of the amount of energy in each frequency. The cortex, found on the outer surface of the brain, has more energy in the higher frequencies than the thalamus, a region located deep in the brain that conveys sensory information to the cortex.

tion of the frequencies and thus a change in the way people perceive the sound. Low frequencies may not be represented well, for instance, so the reproduction sounds too high-pitched, or tinny.

Frequency distortion also occurs in nature. Earth's atmosphere attenuates high-frequency sounds more than low-frequency sounds; that means that high frequencies do not travel as far. A distant thunderstorm, for example, seems different than it does when it finally arrives: from far away the thunder rumbles, but when the storm is directly overhead the thunder accompanying lightning seems to crackle. This is not due to a change in the thunder and lightning, since they are the same whether near or far. What has changed is that the high frequencies from distant thunder are not heard, because the air reduces these frequencies before the sound reaches the listener. As a result, the listener hears a low-frequency rumbling. When lightning strikes nearby, though, the high frequencies in the thunder will not be so greatly reduced, and so the listener hears crackling.

Something similar occurs as sound travels through the walls of an apartment or dormitory. Sound travels through walls because it produces vibrations in the material, which transmit these oscillations to air on the other side. Most construction materials attenuate high frequencies, similarly to air. This means that apartment dwellers cannot hear their neighbor's high-frequency sounds such as speech very well, but they can hear the low-frequency thumping of the drum or bass of their neighbor's radio, even if the volume is low.

An exact reproduction of the music's frequencies is a necessary property of recorders and players that are high-fidelity—"hi-fi," meaning the reproduced sound is close or identical to the original. All of the frequency components should be present in their original intensity and relative strength. People judge amplifiers and speaker equipment by their flat response across the frequency spectrum, meaning that the equipment should not distort the sound by changing its frequency content.

But there are some occasions when musicians not only allow distortion, they deliberately introduce it. Heavy metal musicians create their "metallic" sounds by amplifying electrical signals from their instruments until the signals are distorted. Sine waves become clipped because the amplifier is not able to generate a high enough amplitude to follow the signal faithfully. These waves are no longer pure tones and extra frequencies appear, a process that provides an interesting musical experience, to say the least.

Records and Tapes

Plastic records quickly became popular for machine-recorded music, particularly after the music industry developed a "long-playing" format to allow more music to be recorded on a single record. The grooves became smaller and the record players became more sophisticated. Common types of record were played at a speed of $33^{1}/_{3}$ revolutions per minute (rpm)—the record player revolved $33^{1}/_{3}$ times every minute—and at 45 rpm and 78 rpm. (Small versions of the 45-rpm records were "singles" because each side held only one song, though there was another song on the "flip" or "B" side of the main song.)

As discussed in chapter 3, magnetic tape gradually became a popular *medium* on which to record and play music. On magnetic tape, the electrical representation of the music is not recorded in

Some people refuse to give up their old vinyl records and turntables. *(Kyle Kirkland)*

grooves but in the orientation of small magnetic particles, located in a coating on the surface of a flexible plastic tape. Tape is conveniently small and more portable than records.

But there are problems with magnetic tape. Taped music can be distorted, and unwanted signals called noise can be introduced, so that the sound from a tape player is not nearly a perfect reproduction of the original sound. This was particularly true in the early years of tape recorders, and people could easily distinguish between tape and a live performance. But a discovery by German physicists and engineers during World War II greatly improved the situation—much to the confusion of American and British spies.

The Germans discovered that adding a high-frequency signal of, say, 100,000 hertz to the original recording resulted in a much more accurate reproduction. The 100,000-hertz signal was not present in the original, but this frequency is well above the range of human hearing and so it is not perceived. (A bat could probably hear it but a person cannot.) The process of adding a high-frequency signal is known as biasing. The reason biasing helps is that it makes the alignment of the magnetic particles more closely proportional to the signal that one wants to record. Because of biasing, tape recordings using the best equipment became difficult to distinguish from live performances. Some of the German broadcasts during the war were actually from tape recordings but fooled the Allies, who believed the reproduction was too good to be from tape.

But magnetic tape still has its drawbacks. A small amount of noise called hiss is always present, and both records and tapes, no matter how good their quality, suffer from at least some unwelcome noise. To deal with this, musicians and recording companies in the latter part of the 20th century changed the way they stored music. Instead of an *analog* recording, in which the information is stored as a continuous signal, they switched to a digital format, in which the information is stored as a series of numbers. The sidebar on page 102 explains this process in more detail.

Any medium can store data in digital format, although this format requires a lot of space. Magnetic tapes can hold a digital format, but in general only professionals have used such tapes. The cassette tapes bought by consumers were, and still

Analog versus Digital

In an analog tape recording, the orientation and number of magnetic particles at each point on the tape represent the value, or amplitude, of the recorded signal at that point. If a large number of particles are involved, then the signal at this point is strong (and the sound will be loud). But what if there were a few more particles? The signal should in theory be slightly stronger, but in practice the exact number of particles is not precisely controllable during the recording process. A few more or a few less magnetic particles are correctly oriented at different spots even if the original signal was exactly the same at those places. This is noise—the recorded signal is not a perfect replica of the original. The recording process may also be different for different frequencies, so the frequency content may not be the same.

In a digital recording, the signal is sampled. Sampling means taking the value of the signal at certain points in time. This is different from analog, which uses the whole, continuous signal. Digital signals are stored as numbers that represent their value at these specific times. The sample rate determines the number of times per second that the original signal is sampled. A sample rate of 100 per second means that for 100 times each second—at equally spaced intervals—the recording system measures the value of the original signal and then converts it into a number and stores the series of numbers. The process of converting a continuous signal into a digital one is called digitizing. The figure shows an example.

The advantage of digital recordings is noise reduction. Digital signals can be stored in binary form (the numbers are converted into a string of 1s and 0s), the same way computers store and process data. Codes inserted into the data correct any errors in the numbers so that the machines will read and write with complete accuracy. Whereas analog recordings are "sloppy"—the recording is slightly different from the original—digital recordings are precise. The resulting sound is sharp, with little noise.

The main disadvantage of digital recordings is that they require a lot of storage space in order to hold the huge quantity of numbers. How much space they need depends on the required accuracy and on the sample rate. But this disadvantage is not

are, mostly analog. Digital recordings for consumers did not become popular until the development of compact discs (CDs), which have a huge storage capacity, as described in the next section.

much of a problem because modern digital *media* can hold a lot (see the section on CDs and DVDs).

Another possible disadvantage is a loss of data, because the process of digitizing discards some of the signal. But it turns out that if the sample rate is high enough, then no information in the original signal is lost as a result of digitizing. Although this seems surprising, it is true: a continuous signal can be faithfully reproduced from a limited number of samples if the sample rate is at least twice as high as the highest frequency contained in the original signal's spectrum. The reason is that even though the digitizer only samples the data, if it does so at a high enough rate, then the signal will not change much between samples and nothing important is lost.

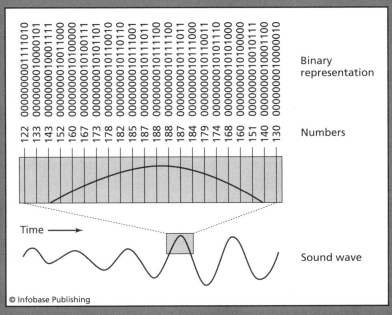

© Infobase Publishing

The bottom part of the figure is the sound wave to be converted into digital format. The top part of the figure shows the digitizing process of a small, highlighted part of the wave. At equally spaced points, the digitizer measures the magnitude of the wave and represents it as a number, which it converts to binary format for storage.

The switch to digital recordings was not the only improvement in the 20th century. As physicists and engineers gained more experience working with records and tapes and the materials from which they are made, these recording media became more sophisticated. The equipment got smaller, and tapes were made with multiple tracks that ran parallel to each other. For instance, magnetic tapes with two tracks could record stereo sound. The term *stereo* refers to the presence of two or more channels and is more lifelike than a sound from a single source, such as a single loudspeaker. This is because sound travels from all directions in most environments and people have two ears, one on each side, so that human brains can compare the different signals from each ear to locate sound sources. Recordings made with four channels, called quadraphonic, made an appearance in the 1970s but did not catch on, apparently failing to add much beyond the effect produced by two channels. But movies with "surround sound," which hit their audience with sounds from all directions, are popular.

Any sound at all is an improvement on the silent movies of the early 20th century. The first movies were silent because although sound could be played from records or cylinders, no one knew how to store sounds on a film. Movies are a series of still pictures on film that give the illusion of motion if the projector shows the film quickly enough. In order to have sound, a record would have to be played that was perfectly matched or synchronized with the film—when a character in the movie opened his mouth, the record would have play the voice at that precise instant; otherwise, everything would look and sound funny.

Synchronization of a record with a film was used for some of the early "talkies," but a better solution occurred when people realized that sounds could be represented on film as strips of variable darkness or variable width. Engineers recorded the sound and stored it on the film itself in a little track off to the side. Light-sensing equipment translated the track data into an electrical signal that was then sent to the speakers. Since the track was on the film itself, synchronization was not a problem and the sound matched what was happening in the movie. These tracks are called soundtracks.

CDs and DVDs

As magnetic tapes became widespread, both music and movies were recorded and stored. As mentioned earlier, tapes are effective but noisy. The arrival of CDs and their digital format changed everything.

A standard CD (compact disc) for audio recording uses a sample rate of 44.1 kilohertz (44,100 samples a second) and stores the numbers in a track spiraling around the disc. The track consists of a series of flat stretches called lands mixed in with tiny pits, which can be smaller than 0.00004 inch (0.0001 cm). Because the pits and lands are so tiny, the track is long, even though the disc itself is small—the spiral wraps around the disc many times. If someone could stretch a CD's spiral track into a straight line it would be more than three miles (4.8 km) long.

The pits and lands encode a series of 1s and 0s, the binary language. (This language is also used for computers, as discussed earlier; therefore, CDs can store computer data as well as music.) Reading a CD requires a concentrated light source. The CD player bounces a light beam off the track, and the amount of reflected light varies, depending on the pit or land. (Sometimes the pits are called bumps—whether the surface indentation is a pit or a bump depends on the side of the disc on which it is viewed.) Light detectors measure the amount of light and then the disc turns, and the player examines the next tiny section. The light beam comes from a small laser, which is narrow and controllable and can illuminate tiny sections of the track.

The disc's pits and lands are so small that they are close to size of the wavelength of light. Although they are impossible to see with the eye, the pits make their presence known by the colored bands reflecting from the back of a CD. These colors are due to interference—some of the reflected wavelengths cancel, leaving colored light. The tiny size of the pits also means that they cannot be made very much smaller and still be read by the player's laser, because light can only reflect from objects and features whose size is at least about as large as its wavelength.

Another digital storage medium is a DVD, which closely resembles a CD in appearance. The pits in a DVD are slightly smaller than those in a CD, but the DVD players can read them because they use a laser that shines with radiation of a smaller wavelength. A DVD can also have several layers sandwiched in the disc. Both of these features mean that DVDs hold more numbers than CDs—DVDs commonly store movies and have begun to replace videocassette tape. According to some people, *DVD* stands for "digital video disk," although this is not an official designation.

Since movies are a series of still pictures (called frames) shown at a high rate, how does a DVD store them? The digital format converts the pictures into numbers—a huge quantity of them. There are so many numbers that even a DVD could not hold them all, and the numbers have to be compressed into a smaller set in order to fit a two-hour movie onto a little disc. Coding is possible because most movies films have 24 frames a second, but some of the objects and information on each frame do not change. A stationary tree may form the background in a scene lasting 10 seconds (240 frames), but it is not necessary for a DVD to include the tree in all 240 frames. The DVD might simply store a digital representation of the tree along with the instructions "This tree is at such and such a place in these frames."

The compression of movies on DVDs means that DVD players not only have to read the track but also must decode the information as the movie is playing. This process requires fast electronics, but a standard way of compressing movies was established by the Moving Picture Experts Group (MPEG), so there is no confusion as to how to interpret the DVD's information. (MP3 players use a similar technique for compressing large music files so that they take up less storage space.)

CDs and DVDs have mostly replaced magnetic tape and vinyl records. But there are some things that the new media cannot do. Hip hop artists continue to use old-fashioned vinyl records, if only to spin and scratch the small grooves to make the interesting sounds that accompany their music—impossible with a CD!

Future Ways to Play Music and Movies

The transition from tapes and records to the digital formats of CDs and DVDs had an important impact on the entertainment industry, but no one knows how long this will last, or what kind of new media the future will introduce. Considering the constant advances in physics and engineering, the only certainty in today's world is change. Although CDs and DVDs are currently popular, so were magnetic tapes and vinyl records in their day. Media of the future will be even better.

Engineers from large electronics companies such as Sony have already developed discs that are similar to DVDs but hold more information. Readers for many of these discs use blue-light lasers, which have a smaller wavelength than lasers used in today's DVD players. The tracks can therefore be smaller and the density of information—the amount of information per area—increases. Blu-ray Discs and high-density DVDs are two examples.

In the more distant future, however, even these discs will probably be replaced by something better: chips. Discs such as CDs, DVDs, and the newer increased-capacity discs are not perfect. They can get scratched, they are somewhat large and awkward (in this era of miniaturization), and disc readers require moving parts that have a tendency to break or wear out. A more effective and convenient medium to store a movie or a huge number of songs is a chip the size of an integrated circuit.

Smaller-capacity, relatively slow chips are already available. These chips, called flash memory, are commonly found in digital cameras, mobile phones, MP3 players, and memory cards for small computers. For example, they are in some versions of Apple Computer's iPod, a popular device that stores and plays songs. (Other iPod models use small hard disk drives, similar to the storage medium of computers.) Flash memory stores information in an array of cells consisting of transistors. The memory retains the information even after power is turned off, unlike, say, the random access memory (RAM) of computers. There are limitations to the flash memory devices of today—they do not have a sufficiently high density or speed to provide an inexpensive medium to handle the huge amount of data contained in movies.

But physics continues to move forward, and flash memories that can do the job—or something else that can do an even better job—will emerge soon. The physics of electromagnetism has introduced a world full of sound and moving pictures into people's homes. The wax cylinders of the late 19th century stored only a few seconds of speech, but they proved to be a good start, a step toward today's discs, which hold entire movies and more. These too are temporary, a small step toward materials and technology that future physicists and engineers will discover.

8

ELECTRICITY, MAGNETISM, AND LIFE

M ARY WOLLSTONECRAFT SHELLEY published a novel in 1818 that would become one of the most famous stories of all time: *Frankenstein, or The Modern Prometheus,* is the story of a scientist, Victor Frankenstein, who discovers how to instill life into nonliving material. He creates a life-form—Frankenstein's monster—but matters turn out badly, and the monster destroys him. The tragic story has been the subject of numerous horror movies and television shows over the years.

Although Shelley did not specify in the novel exactly how Victor Frankenstein brought his monster to life, most of the movies have made use of the strong relationship between life and the physics of electricity. The monster is usually shown receiving the spark of life from lightning, a powerful electrical phenomenon. In a dramatic scene with crackling thunder and flashes of lightning bolts striking the castle laboratory, the monster comes to life.

Hollywood often fails to portray science with any accuracy, but the use of the electricity as the spark of life is a reasonable one. Electricity and magnetism have long been known to be involved in biological processes, and the principles of physics are the same whether they are at work in inanimate (nonliving) matter or living beings. As mentioned in chapter 1, all of the ancient civilizations were familiar with electric fish, though these animals were poorly understood at first. Gradually scientists gained an understanding of how electricity works in animals, and in humans also.

Electric Animals

In the late 18th and early 19th centuries, around the same time that Shelley wrote *Frankenstein,* physicists and physiologists were studying electricity and living tissues. The Italian physiologist Luigi Galvani (1737–98) sent electric current through the nerves and muscles of frog legs and watched them twitch. On the basis of these and other experiments, Galvani claimed that life and motion were powered by "animal electricity." Other experimenters demonstrated this idea not only in animals but also in humans. Some of the human experiments, though disturbing, pointed to a role of electricity in the movement of human limbs and muscles. Electric shocks through the corpses of hanged criminals caused the limbs to twitch and shake, and if the current was strong enough the whole body did a ghastly dance, as if somehow life had returned along with the current. Many scientists and onlookers found these experiments repugnant but intriguing.

Electricity's role in life became better understood when people finally understood the *cell,* the basic component of life. All organisms are composed of one or more fluid-filled cells, each of which is usually about 0.002 inch (0.005 cm) in size. The fluid is water, but with a lot of different substances dissolved in it. The human body consists of trillions of cells of different kinds—brain cells, kidney cells, skin cells, muscle cells, and so on. The cells are surrounded by another fluid, which is different in composition from that of the fluid inside the cell. A thin *membrane,* composed of large molecules of protein and lipids (fat), envelops each cell and separates the interior fluid from the exterior.

Cells or networks of connected cells govern the processes normally associated with life—respiration, metabolism, and motion. Organs and systems are collections of cells working together. Another feature of cells—a property that is quite surprising—is that cells have an electric potential across their membrane. The existence of this voltage means that an electric charge placed either inside or outside the cell will be pushed across the membrane, if there is a path (a conductor) in which it can move.

This voltage puzzled scientists at first. There are plenty of charges, called ions, floating around in the fluids both inside and

Ions and Ion Channels

Some compounds, such as sodium chloride (table salt) or potassium chloride, dissolve in water. In the case of dissolved sodium chloride, the bond between sodium and chloride breaks and the two atoms separate. While connected the two atoms share an electron, but when the sodium chloride splits the electron goes with the chloride, giving it a negative charge. As a result of the absence of the electron in the sodium atom there is one extra proton in the sodium atom's nucleus, so this atom has a positive charge. These charged atoms floating around in water are ions.

Seawater is salty—it has a lot of dissolved salt, with many ions of various kinds, and these ions make salty water an electrical conductor. There are also a lot of ions in the fluids inside and outside the cells of an animal's body, but the concentrations—the amount per volume of fluid—are different in the inside and outside solutions. For example, the inside of the cell has a much higher concentration of potassium ions, and the outside of the cell has a much higher concentration of sodium ions.

Ions can move through the membrane, but only through special proteins called *ion channels.* A protein is a large molecule composed of smaller molecules called amino acids strung together like beads on a necklace; proteins fold into a certain geometrical shape in order to perform their function, and ion channels fold themselves into a shape that makes a hole in the membrane through which ions can travel. But ions can only flow through channels that are open, and most channels are not always open. Furthermore, ion channels tend to pass only one type of ion—there are ion channels that let sodium ions pass but tend to block potassium and other ions, and other channels that do the opposite.

outside the membrane, and ions can move through the fluid to make a current. But the membrane is composed of materials that do not conduct electricity, so how did the voltage arise and what is its function? As discussed in the sidebar, the answer is that there are channels for ions to flow through, and these channels help create the membrane potential of cells.

The membrane potential arises because there are slightly more negative ions inside the cell and slightly more positive ions outside. The difference in concentrations between the inside and outside of the cell causes this inequality. For example, because there are more potassium ions inside the cell than outside, potassium ions have a strong tendency to flow outside. But as potassium ions flow through the channels, this process leads to an accumulation of positive charges outside, causing a voltage across the membrane. The voltage of the outside is positive with respect to the inside (which means the inside is negative), and by Coulomb's law this exerts an attractive electrical force on the positively charged potassium ions to keep them inside. All of the other types of ion flow through their channels and contribute to the potential in a similar way. As a result, a potential in which there is no more net flow of charges across the cell's membrane develops. This is the equilibrium potential, and it is maintained unless changes occur to the ion channels or in the ion concentrations.

Proteins such as ion channels are too small to be seen by eye or even with a light microscope. No one knew ion channels existed until scientists found them in the 20th century, when physiologists such as Sir Alan Lloyd Hodgkin (1914–98) and Sir Andrew Fielding Huxley (1917–) studied membranes by using sensitive current-measuring devices and other electrical equipment to detect the flow of ions through them. These two British scientists won a share of the 1963 Nobel Prize in physiology for their work. Because electricity is so important to biology, ion channels continue to be studied. Roderick MacKinnon, at the Rockefeller University in New York, won a share of the 2003 Nobel Prize in chemistry for determining the three-dimensional structure of the hole or "pore" in a specific type of ion channel.

The electrical properties of cells are a major part of biophysics—the study of the physics of biological systems. The voltage across a cell's membrane is tiny, often about 60 or 70 millivolts (thousandths of a volt). Even a small battery is hundreds of times stronger. But this small potential can have large effects on a biological cell. The reason is that the membrane is thin, only about 0.00000016–0.00000032 inch (0.0000004–0.0000008 cm), and although the voltage is small, it is exerted across an extremely thin material, so the voltage per unit distance is huge. Anything con-

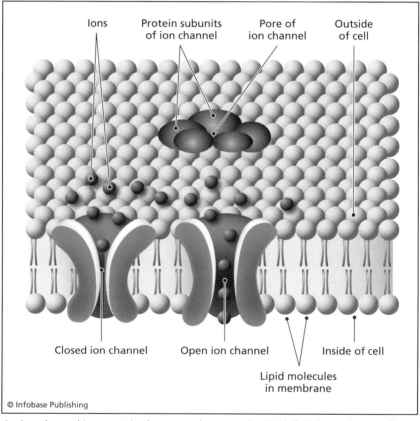

Ions
Protein subunits of ion channel
Pore of ion channel
Outside of cell

Closed ion channel
Open ion channel
Inside of cell
Lipid molecules in membrane

© Infobase Publishing

An ion channel is a protein that extends across the lipid (fatty) membrane of a cell. The membrane consists of two layers of lipid molecules, with their heads (round part) facing the water solution inside and outside the cell. Embedded in this membrane are ion channels that, when open, allow the passage of ions, which cannot otherwise get across the lipid layers.

tained in the membrane feels a powerful electrical force, and this includes the proteins that form ion channels. The figure on page 112 shows a diagram of an ion channel.

The powerful electrical force makes its presence felt. Membranes are insulators and have few if any mobile charges, but the amino acids that compose proteins can and do have charges. Some of the ion channel proteins have charges that sense the membrane potential, and such ion channels are called voltage-sensitive channels. The electrical force exerted across the membrane in which they are embedded causes these proteins to fold into a certain shape, and changes in the membrane potential change the shape. The change in shape can turn an open channel into a closed channel, or the converse. In this way, the membranes of muscles, nerves, brain cells, and heart cells have electrical excitability—they are responsive to voltages and currents. Galvani and the other early experimenters discovered this when they sent electric currents into nerves and muscles and observed the twitches. Although Galvani knew nothing about ion channels (which had not been discovered yet), he did realize that the physics of electricity is very much involved in biological tissues.

The opening and closing of ion channels cause a current to flow across the membrane, which temporarily changes the potential. The cells of electric fish do it often, producing an electric shock when they discharge. Some species of electric fish stun their prey with these shocks, and other species use electricity as a sort of radar to "see" their environment (particularly where the water is murky and normal vision is ineffective). Each cell's membrane potential is only tens of millivolts, so it would not seem that the fish could generate much electricity, but this is not true. Cells in these fish form a series circuit (discussed in the sidebar on electric circuits in chapter 1). Since this is the type of circuit in which voltages add together, the sum of the huge number of these cells can deliver a strong punch.

Electricity of the Muscle

Electrical discharges occur in other animals or in other tissues that are similar to those of electric fish but are milder and have a different function. A discharge in a muscle cell causes the cell to contract. This is the twitching that Galvani saw, invoked by his electrical equipment. But the contractions are also the means by which animals normally move.

Muscles are electrically excitable tissues—they can generate electrical discharges called *action potentials.* Muscles do not send electrical currents into the environment as electrical fish do, but instead they have special proteins and other molecules that cause them to shorten as a result of an action potential. As it contracts, the muscle pulls on the bone to which it is connected (actually the muscle pulls on a tendon, which in turn is connected to the bone), and this action creates a force.

Sensitive equipment can record the electrical activity of muscles. Scientists and physicians sometimes record the discharges directly from the muscle cell but more often paste large electrodes on the skin near the muscle. The electrodes sense the electric currents caused by the discharges of nearby muscles. The process of recording the electrical activity of muscles is called electromyography (*myo* refers to muscle and *graph* means writing), and produces an *electromyogram* (EMG).

Physicians use the EMG to see whether anything is wrong with the muscle's electrical processes, and scientists use the EMG to study how the body works. There is usually always some muscle "tone"—at least a few muscles are always active; otherwise the body would go completely limp. Even standing or sitting requires muscular effort to withstand the force of gravity. The one exception to this rule occurs during a period of sleep known as rapid eye movement (REM) sleep, when all of the body's muscles relax. REM sleep is associated with dreaming because people often report dreaming during this period. The EMG is flat during REM sleep, since there is no activity and the body is limp and will not move. Perhaps the reason a person loses muscle tone during REM sleep is so that he or she is not able to get up and act out the dream!

Since action potentials can only cause a contraction, muscles cannot push against anything. In order to produce complex movements muscles have to work together. When a lot of muscles must be active at once—for instance, when an ice skater performs a triple axel or a basketball player tries a jump shot—all of these muscles must be coordinated, or the person will make an awkward and ineffective movement. Coordination is the job of nerves, which originate in the nervous system. Nerves that coordinate movement are bundles of fibers running from the brain and spinal cord to the muscles of the body.

Nerves use the same sort of electrical discharges—action potentials—that muscles do, though these discharges do not serve the same purpose. Action potentials in nerves carry a message that tells the muscle to produce its own action potential, which in the muscle triggers a contraction. In the brain, there is a "map" of the body's muscles, with nerves leading to muscles in each region of the body. Action potentials traveling in nerves are the brain's way of sending messages to activate this muscle or that muscle, so that the right muscle contracts at the right time. This is yet another way that the physics of electricity performs a biological function: the discharges can send out shocks in electric fish, cause contractions in muscles, and send messages in nerves. Although early scientists such as Galvani were mistaken in many of the details of their theories, electricity performs a number of critical jobs in biology. The list of jobs is discussed further in the next two sections, which examine the heart and brain.

Interruption of the message pathway from the nervous system to the muscles may have a dire consequence, paralysis. The muscles are not able to generate an action potential (which leads to a contraction) on their own because they require a triggering message from the nervous system (or from some source of current, such as that from the equipment used by Galvani). When the pathway is severed, then no more messages are forthcoming, and the muscles no longer contract. The loss of nerves, such as a break in the spinal cord due to an accident or a serious fall, causes a loss in the ability to move on one's own.

Sometimes nerves grow back, but this is not the case for the nerves in the spinal cord. Although biologists are working on a method to heal severed spinal cords, there is perhaps another way of mending the damage that bypasses the injury. The muscles need messages to tell them to contract at the right time, so perhaps the job could be done by supplying those messages from electrical circuits devised to take the place of nerves. The circuits must be fast and deliver messages, in the form of electrical discharges, at the right time and place, but this is nothing extraordinary—electrical circuits can be used to help fly a complicated fighter jet, and they are quick enough and complex enough to work human muscles. The problem in making such a device work is the means of controlling it. The paralyzed person can no longer direct the muscle by thinking about it, as does an uninjured person, but soon there may exist circuits that can interpret the brain's activity and translate it into commands to the muscles. These devices, if they can be built, would bridge the gap of a severed spinal cord and allow a paralyzed person's nervous system to control his or her muscles again. Such devices are not available today, but there is no law in physics or biology that precludes their creation.

Electricity of the Heart

The heart is a muscle, but it is a special one. Although the heart has ion channels similar to those in skeletal muscles (muscles that are attached to bones), the contractions do not move the body, but rather the blood. As with an EMG, electrodes pasted on the skin can record the electrical activity of the heart, a process called electrocardiography, which produces a record called an *electrocardiogram,* abbreviated ECG (*cardio* means heart). (An older abbreviation is *EKG,* which used a German version of the word in honor of the country where the technique began.)

The heart has a rhythm or beat, so the electrical activity is periodic. In humans, the heart has four chambers that work together to pump blood through the blood vessels. Each chamber contracts at a specific time during the heartbeat, and the whole muscle works efficiently and, for most people, reliably. If a patient presents any signs of heart disease, physicians perform an ECG; the result can reveal abnormal rhythms or problems in the blood supply to the heart itself, and the condition of the heart muscle. On the basis of the findings of the ECG, the physician might order other tests to study the problem further.

The heart's rhythm varies during the course of the day, and a part of the nervous system called the autonomic nervous system influences the rate. Exercise raises the rate because active muscles need more blood, and if a person is nervous the heart also beats faster (in anticipation of the possible need to run). But in any case there should be a smooth rhythm, and problems can arise if the heart continually beats too fast, too slowly, or irregularly (in which case the interval between beats is not consistent, or the activity is not what it should be).

Each heartbeat begins with an electrical discharge at a particular place of the heart called the sinoatrial node. This area is also called the pacemaker, because it sets or makes the pace of the heart rhythm. The electrical activity and the specific properties of the ion channels of the pacemaker are crucial to the functioning of the heart, and if they are not working properly the heart may show an arrhythmia, an abnormal heart rhythm. Parts of the heart other than the pacemaker can also produce arrhythmias if they do not activate in their correct sequence.

In some cases arrhythmias are not harmful, and in other cases medication can help. But sometimes an arrhythmia needs further attention, and an understanding of the physics of electricity—along with the development of sophisticated electronics—comes to the aid of modern medicine. One such aid is a cardiac pacemaker. Some people call these devices artificial pacemakers to distinguish them from the heart's natural pacemaker (sinoatrial node).

An artificial pacemaker is a small electrical device that stimulates the heart of a patient. Physicians usually implant the pacemaker in the patient's chest wall, above the muscles and bones of the chest. The pacemaker guides the rhythm of the heart, providing a small jolt of electricity to set the pace. Often the problem that pacemakers are meant to fix is a slow heart rate—the heart is not beating fast enough.

Although pacemakers have been built since the 1950s, the earliest models were not implanted in the body. But with the development of tiny electronic components such as the transistor,

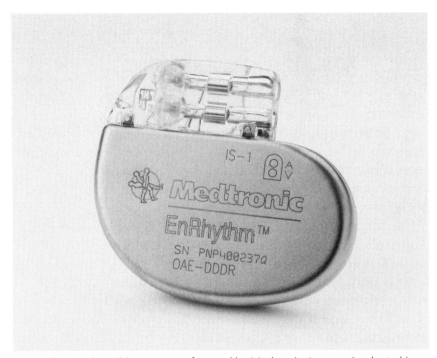

Pacemakers such as this one, manufactured by Medtronic, Inc., are implanted in the chest and stimulate the heart with electricity. These devices help maintain a steady rhythm in patients whose heart is not functioning properly. *(Medtronic, Inc.)*

pacemakers quickly became small and implantable. Advances in battery technology allow pacemakers to run a long time before they need to be replaced, saving the patient from frequent surgery—batteries in pacemakers implanted in the early 1960s had a life of about 18 months, whereas today they can last more than a decade. Pacemakers are quite common today, and several million patients have received pacemaker implants since 1960. Pacemakers are tough and reliable, but patients still need to be careful, because strong magnetic or electric fields can interfere with pacemaker function. Magnetic resonance imaging (MRI), for instance, can cause serious trouble.

Another electronic device useful in medical situations is the defibrillator. A defibrillator uses a jolt of electricity to restart a stopped heart. On certain occasions, especially in people with heart disease, the cardiac muscle gets so out of synchronization

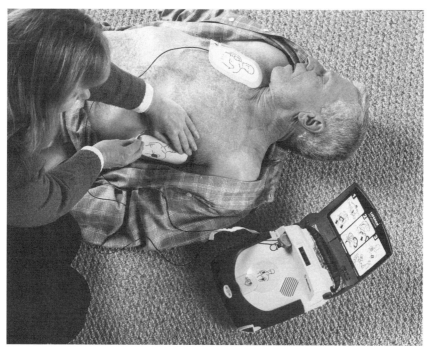

When a heart suddenly stops as a result of fibrillation—a form of cardiac arrest or heart attack—a device called a defibrillator shocks the heart muscle into a normal rhythm again. Electrodes placed on the chest deliver the electric current. *(Medtronic, Inc.)*

that the heart simply quivers. This is a fibrillation. When a fibrillation occurs in the part of the heart called the ventricles (ventricular fibrillation), this is a medical emergency because the heart is no longer pumping blood. A defibrillator consists of electrodes that are placed on the patient's chest and an electric generator to provide a surge of current. The current must be quite strong and is a rare exception to the rule that electrical shock is harmful. In defibrillation, the jolt of electricity often (though not always) causes the heart to restart a normal rhythm, inducing a badly misfiring heart to "reset" itself.

Electricity of the Brain

Cardiac and skeletal muscle use electricity, and as Galvani and other scientists discovered, electricity is also critical in the operation of the nerves. Nerves are the pathways for information traveling to and from the brain, and therefore it seemed to early scientists in Galvani's time that electricity must also play a role in the brain's functioning. They were correct.

Electric currents due to ions and ion channels are crucial to brain cells called *neurons*. Neurons generate action potentials similar to those of cardiac and skeletal muscle cells, though the brain's action potentials do not cause its cells to contract. In the brain and the rest of the nervous system, action potentials are used for communication: neurons send messages to each other and to other cells of the body in the form of action potentials. (Some of the other cells that neurons communicate with are muscle cells, and as mentioned earlier, this communication occurs through the nerves. A nerve consists of a bundle of long, thin projections of neurons.)

The brain is an excellent information processor, taking in information and acting upon it by orchestrating the body's response,

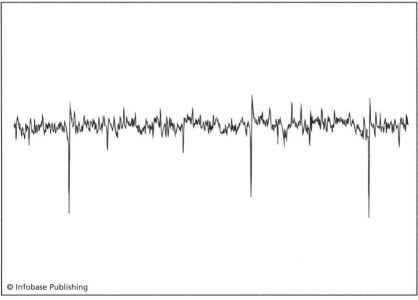

© Infobase Publishing

This is an electrical recording from the brain stem of a mouse. The three spikes are action potentials of a single cell as it sends messages to other cells in the brain. (Kyle Kirkland)

in the form movement (contraction of muscles) or some other action. Sensory organs such as the eye and ear encode events in the world into trains of action potentials, and certain neurons in the brain send messages in the form of action potentials to muscles in order to direct movement. Action potentials are the language of the brain: they code information in terms of their rate (how many occur per second) or in terms of their timing (when they occur in relation to other action potentials).

The brain contains billions of neurons, many of which are active at the same time. It is an electrically active place and numerous tiny currents are flowing at any given instant. A small amount of this current leaks across the skull and scalp; recording this current with electrodes pasted on the scalp is called electro-encephalograpy (*cephalo* refers to the head) and produces an *electroencephalogram* (EEG). An EEG is a recording of thousands of neural conversations, all mixed together. Scientists would love to be able to decode and understand these conversations, but at the present time no one knows exactly what all these neurons "say" to each other as they process information. Studying the EEG has been likened to putting a single microphone in a loud stadium and trying to understand the game from nothing but the noise. A listener can hear the roar of the crowd and conclude that an important event just occurred, but the nature and details of the event are not clear.

Despite the limited information, EEGs are important because they let scientists and physicians study the electrical activity of the brain without having to open up the skull. (Other ways to study the brain include imaging devices such as the fMRI discussed earlier, but these devices do not record the electrical activity directly. Imaging is also extremely expensive compared to the EEG.) Physicians often use EEGs to study seizure disorders, for example. A seizure is a runaway electrical excitation of the brain in which millions of neurons suddenly stop their useful conversations and instead produce action potentials at the same time. Waves of activity roll through the brain, sometimes causing a convulsion as neurons send inappropriate messages to the muscles. Seizure disorders are common, affecting about 1 percent of the population.

Abnormal activity shows up on the EEG during a seizure and, in some patients, at other times as well.

Neural messages are scrambled during seizures as a result of the unusual level of activity, but in other situations the messages do not work because the communication links are broken. For instance, deafness will occur with the death of sensory cells of the inner ear that transform sound waves into trains of action potentials. Neurons cannot act on information they do not receive. Deafness is similar to paralysis in that the information pathway is severed.

But the development of sophisticated electronics, thanks to an understanding of the physics of electricity, can help alleviate some of these problems. Unlike paralysis, for which not much can be done as yet, electronic devices already exist to help a large fraction of hearing-impaired people to hear again. A cochlear implant, placed in the inner ear, is one such device. Cochlear implants work by transforming sound waves into pulses of electricity and conveying these pulses to neurons. The implant bridges the gap in the communication link caused by the death of sensory neurons. Only a small number of electrodes—a dozen or so—can be surgically placed, and this small number cannot fully compensate for the loss of the approximately 15,000 sensory cells that normally do the job. But the patient can hear sound, sometimes well enough to understand speech. About 60,000 people in the world have received cochlear implants.

The transfer of information accomplished by cochlear implants is relatively simple—the presence of a sound wave and an approximation of its frequency. Other information processing done by the brain is a lot more complicated, and scientists do not understand it. At the present time, only simple circuits that can mimic aspects of the information processing capacity of the brain exist. These circuits are sometimes called artificial neural networks, named after the real networks of neurons in the brain that process information. Artificial neural networks have been used for recognition of handwritten characters and in the finding of patterns in complex situations, tasks at which computers perform poorly but the human brain excels.

As the second and third chapters of this book showed, the physics of electricity is strongly related to magnetism. The same must be true of the brain, since the laws of physics work here as they do everywhere else. If the laws of physics are correct, then all of those electric currents in the brain should produce a magnetic field—and they do. The magnetic field is small, only about a billionth of the strength of Earth's magnetic field, but it exists and can be measured by a sensitive piece of electronics called a SQUID (discussed in chapter 6).

The study of magnetic fields of the brain is not as common as EEG but it provides another way of watching the brain in action. Not only does the brain generate a magnetic field, it can also be affected by one (this again is in accordance with the laws of physics). Scientists use large magnetic fields to stimulate the brain by inducing currents in the neurons. In one type of experiment, magnetic fields temporarily and harmlessly turn off specific parts of a person's brain. The goal of this kind of experiment is to find out what those parts of the brain do by examining a person's behavior when the parts are shut down—if a certain type of behavior such as visual perception changes, then scientists infer that the part in question must contribute to this behavior. Physicians are also testing magnetic fields to determine whether they may have beneficial effects in the treatment of disorders such as depression.

But there are limits to the electricity and magnetism of the brain. Some people have claimed that electrical or magnetic stimulation of the brain can produce wonderful effects such as vastly increased learning skills and total relaxation. There is no scientific basis for these claims.

And yet the presence of electromagnetic phenomena in the brain raises interesting questions. Many animals seem to have an instinct for direction and navigation, and a few of them are uncanny in their ability to find their way around. People have realized that some of these animals might be carrying an internal compass.

Animals with Built-in Compasses

Some animals are great navigators. Many bird species travel long distances every year, commonly migrating from harsh winter conditions to a warmer climate where food is more abundant. Arctic terns are an extreme case, traveling more than 10,000 miles (16,000 km) from their arctic breeding grounds to spend the winter in the Southern Hemisphere. Sea turtles also travel great distances, as do certain species of fish. Homing pigeons can find their way back home even when released in unfamiliar territory. How the animals accomplish these feats of navigation is not always obvious.

These animals undoubtedly use many clues. Landmarks, winds, the position of the Sun and stars are all possible navigational aids for birds. The sense of smell is important to animals such as fish. But Earth's magnetic field also provides a sense of direction that has been used by compass-wielding people for hundreds of years. Earth's magnetic field is an excellent aid because it is always present, day or night, and in all conditions. Do certain animals have a built-in compass?

This is really two questions. Do these animals have a magnetic sense? And do they actually use it for navigation?

The answer to the first question seems to be yes in many cases. Some animals sense magnetic fields and are able to orient them-

The spiny lobster finds its way around at least in part by using Earth's magnetic field. (NOAA/OAR/NURP)

selves using the direction of a magnetic field. This sense is called *magnetoreception.* Several species of birds, loggerhead sea turtles, spiny lobsters, mole rats, salmon, rainbow trout, and even certain kinds of bacteria have magnetoreception.

Magnetoreception acts as any other sense does, with the detection of the sensory phenomenon—in this case, magnetic fields. This may be accomplished by several different methods. Electromagnetic induction is one way, and chemical reactions that are governed by magnetic fields are another. But the best evidence suggests that magnetoreception is often based on the same principle as a compass: animals have tiny crystals of the magnetic mineral magnetite (Fe_3O_4) in their bodies that respond to Earth's magnetic field. Biologists have found magnetite crystals in the head of birds, for example. Magnetite has also been found in honeybees, sea turtles, salmon, and other animals known to have magnetoreception.

The second question is harder to answer. Do the animals actually use magnetoreception to navigate? Presumably the sense of magnetoreception is used in some way; otherwise it would not exist. But proving conclusively that some species of animals do in fact use magnetoreception for navigation is not easy. All animals rely on a number of clues to guide them, and it is difficult for experimenters to show specifically that one or another clue is being used—when one clue is removed, another may be able to compensate. Experiments have shown that the presence of distorting magnetic fields disrupts navigation in certain birds, but other birds do not seem to be affected. Other experiments suggest that loggerhead sea turtles and spiny lobsters at least partially depend on Earth's magnetic field for orientation and navigation. Although research continues, some kind of compass "sense" appears to be at work under a variety of conditions and in a number of species.

Since certain animals have magnetoreception, one can ask whether people have a magnetic sense. Some people have an uncanny sense of direction, so the question is relevant. But there is no evidence that humans have magnetoreception. For humans, finding one's way around in a new place is probably more a matter of spatial and geometric skills.

Electricity and magnetism affect people in plenty of other ways, as this chapter has shown. The circulation of blood, muscular contraction and movement, sensation and perception, even thinking and consciousness depend on the physics of electromagnetism. An understanding of the biological uses of electricity and magnetism has come slowly, but the physics is the same as and is no less important than it is in the rest of the world. Electromagnetism is truly the spark of life.

CONCLUSION

ELECTRICITY AND MAGNETISM play so many roles in today's world that it might be hard to imagine a time when they would become even more important. Yet that time may be soon, and in the future electricity and magnetism may change people and the way they live in even more dramatic ways.

The electrical nature of human and animal muscles, hearts, and brains has been studied since the time of the 18th-century scientist Luigi Galvani, but with the increasing sophistication and miniaturization of electronics, people may soon have an unprecedented ability to act on this knowledge. Pacemakers—devices first developed in the 1950s that use electricity to correct an abnormal rhythm in the heart—may be an early example of things to come. Pacemakers for the brain may arrive in the not too distant future.

Brains sometimes need pacemakers for the same reason that hearts do—as mentioned in chapter 8, seizure disorders, caused by runaway neural excitation, affect about 1 percent of the world's population. Drugs can correct the abnormal rhythms in many patients, but a third of the people suffering from a seizure disorder show little improvement. Electronic devices that detect a seizure and apply electricity to prevent it would work similarly to heart pacemakers, but this is a more difficult task because unlike abnormal heart rhythms, brain seizures are usually episodic (they come and go) and do not generally have pronounced warning signs. But scientists such as Brian Litt at the University of Pennsylvania and Miguel Nicolelis at Duke University have already made machines that, although not quite ready for widespread use, show promise in tests performed in animals and in some human patients.

The development of personal electronics—electrical devices that interface or make connections with the human body and brain—seems likely to occur in a number of different ways. Personal electronics would go beyond the convenient cell phone, or wearable televisions made from organic LEDs, for in the future such devices will be integrated, not separate from the user. Bionic limbs and devices, as portrayed in futuristic television shows and movies, would certainly use electricity as the means of communication between body and machine and provide freedom of movement for those with severe paralytic and arthritic disorders. Bionics may also be used for augmentation—not just to recover lost strength but to add more—in order for people to perform in extraordinary circumstances or environments, such as during the exploration of space.

But perhaps there will be at least a few people in the future who will not feel a need for personal electronics and who may even find such devices too intrusive. The same is true today with portable communication, as there are people, including the author of this book, who manage to survive quite well without a cell phone or instant messaging.

Personal electronics is not the only possible development for electricity and magnetism. The first people who rubbed amber and wool and observed the strange effects could not have imagined the events that would follow their early adventure into electromagnetism. It may also be impossible for people today to imagine what the future of electromagnetism holds, because physics and its applications probably have many more surprises ahead.

SI Units and Conversions

Unit	Quantity	Symbol	Conversion
Base Units			
meter	length	m	1 m = 3.28 feet
kilogram	mass	kg	
second	time	s	
ampere	electric current	A	
Kelvin	thermodynamic temperature	K	1 K = 1°C = 1.8°F
candela	luminous intensity	cd	
mole	amount of substance	mol	
Supplementary Units			
radian	plane angle	rad	π rad = 180 degrees
Derived Units (combinations of base or supplementary units)			
coulomb	electric charge	C	
cubic meter	volume	m^3	1 m^3 = 1,000 liters = 264 gallons
farad	capacitance	F	
henry	inductance	H	

Unit	Quantity	Symbol	Conversion
Derived Units (continued)			
hertz	frequency	Hz	1 Hz = 1 cycle per second
meter/second	speed	m/s	1 m/s = 2.24 miles/hour
Newton	force	N	4.4482 N = 1 pound
Ohm	electric resistance	Ω	
Pascal	pressure	Pa	101,325 Pa = 1 atmosphere
radian/second	angular speed	rad/s	π rad/s = 180 degrees/second
Tesla	magnetic flux density	T	
volt	electromotive force	V	
Watt	power	W	746 W = 1 horsepower

UNIT PREFIXES

Prefixes alter the value of the unit

Example: kilometer = 10^3 meters (1,000 meters)

Prefix	Multiplier	Symbol
femto	10^{-15}	f
pico	10^{-12}	p
nano	10^{-9}	n
micro	10^{-6}	µ
milli	10^{-3}	m
centi	10^{-2}	c
deci	10^{-1}	d
deca	10	da
hecto	10^2	h
kilo	10^3	k
mega	10^6	M
giga	10^9	G
tera	10^{12}	T

GLOSSARY

AC *See* ALTERNATING CURRENT

action potential a brief rise and fall in the membrane potential of biological cells, which in muscle cells leads to a contraction and in brain cells is the means of influencing or communicating with other cells

alternating current an electric current that periodically reverses in direction

analog a continuous quantity, having a numerical value at each instant

capacitance the capability, such as by two separated metal plates, of storing electric charge, equal to charge divided by the voltage

cathode ray tube a sealed tube in which electrons strike a phosphor-coated screen, causing it to emit light

CD *See* COMPACT DISC

cell in biology, the basic unit of life, consisting of a membrane surrounding an aqueous solution of biological molecules and associated structures

central processing unit a computer component that performs the basic operations

charge a particle that gives rise to an electric field and interacts with other such particles as described by Coulomb's law

circuit, parallel a circuit in which there is two or more paths for current to flow

circuit, series a circuit in which there is only one path for current to flow

conductor a material that readily permits a current to flow

compact disc a storage medium for music or computer data

Coulomb's law the law stating that the electrostatic force between two charges is equal to the product of the two quantities of charge divided by the square of the distance separating them; charges of the same sign (positive or negative) repel, charges of different sign attract

CPU *See* CENTRAL PROCESSING UNIT

CRT *See* CATHODE RAY TUBE

crystal a substance having a patterned, geometric arrangement of its component atoms, ions, or molecules

current a flow of electric charge

DC *See* DIRECT CURRENT

digital a quantity, measurement, or signal represented by a series of discrete numbers; an analog signal can be converted into a digital one by sampling its value at periodic intervals

diode a semiconductor allowing charge to move through it in only one direction

direct current an electric current that flows in one direction

DVD a disc that can store a large amount of computer data or video; there is no consensus on what, if anything, the letters stand for

ECG *See* ELECTROCARDIOGRAM

EEG *See* ELECTROENCEPHALOGRAM

electric charge *See* CHARGE

electric current *See* CURRENT

electric field a region in space at which a charge will experience an electrostatic force of a certain magnitude and direction

electrocardiogram a recording of the electrical activity of the heart; the recording process is called electrocardiography

electrode a conductor used to measure or deliver an electric current or voltage

electroencephalogram a recording of the electrical activity of the brain; the recording process is called electroencephalography

electromagnet a temporary and switchable magnet, consisting of a coil of wire that is usually wrapped around an iron core; the coil becomes a magnet when current flows through the wire

electromagnetic induction the process by which a changing magnetic field induces a current in a conductor

electromyogram a recording of the electrical activity of a muscle; the recording process is called electromyography

electron an atomic particle having a negative charge; currents flowing in many conductors, such as metals, consist primarily of electrons in motion

electrostatic force the force that electric charges exert on one another

EMG *See* ELECTROMYOGRAM

Faraday's law The law that states that in electromagnetic induction, the amount of voltage induced is proportional to the rate of change of the magnetic field

ferromagnetism the aligning of the magnetic domains of certain materials, called ferromagnetic, by which the material becomes magnetic

floating point operations per second a general performance measure of a computer's speed

FLOPS *See* FLOATING POINT OPERATIONS PER SECOND

ground, electrical zero potential; often the term *ground* refers to a conductor sunk into the earth in order to carry off any excess charge

hertz unit of frequency equal to one cycle per second

HEV *See* HYBRID ELECTRIC VEHICLE

hybrid electric vehicle having an engine that gets its power from both gasoline combustion and electricity

IC *See* INTEGRATED CIRCUIT

inductance the generation of a voltage in a coil of wire when a time-varying current flows through it

insulator a material that is a poor conductor of electricity

integrated circuit the circuit elements that reside on a thin wafer of a semiconductor material

ion an electrically charged particle

ion channel a protein that spans a cell's membrane and allows the passage of ions

LCD *See* LIQUID CRYSTAL DISPLAY

LED *See* LIGHT-EMITTING DIODE

light-emitting diode semiconductor that emits light and is used in displays and indicators

liquid crystal display used in many computer monitors and televisions

maglev magnetic levitation, the use of magnetic fields to resist gravity; a train that uses magnetic levitation is often simply called a maglev

magnetic domain a uniform magnetic region in a material; in ferromagnetic materials, domains may align to produce a magnet

magnetic field a region in space at which a magnet will experience a force of a certain magnitude and direction

magnetic pole every known magnet has two poles, North and South, that exert a force on any other magnet in the vicinity

magnetic resonance imaging a technique used to image parts of the body

magnetoreception a sense possessed by certain animals of the presence and orientation of magnetic fields

media plural of *medium; see* MEDIUM

medium a substance or material through which an action occurs or information is conveyed; air is the medium for sound, cassette tapes and CDs are media for music

membrane, cell a bilayer (two layers) composed mostly of fats and a little protein that surrounds a biological cell; the membrane prevents the cell's contents from escaping into the surrounding fluid and controls what substances may enter or leave the cell

MRI *See* MAGNETIC RESONANCE IMAGING

natural frequency the frequency in which a body or system tends to oscillate when it is set in motion

neuron a brain cell; most neurons are connected together to form networks and communicate by way of action potentials

Ohm's law although it does not apply to every material, this law states that the voltage across a circuit element equals the product of its resistance and the current flowing through it

parallel circuit *See* CIRCUIT, PARALLEL

potential difference voltage; a difference in potential between two points means that a current will flow in a conductor between those points

RAM *See* RANDOM ACCESS MEMORY

random access memory a common type of memory that a computer uses to hold the programs it is running and the required data

resistance the opposition to a flow of current

resonance the increased response of a system when acted upon or driven by a process having the same frequency as the system's natural frequency

semiconductor a material that can become a conductor with the application of a small amount of voltage

series circuit *See* CIRCUIT, SERIES

spectrum the frequency composition of a waveform or oscillation

superconductor a material that at some well-defined temperature loses all electrical resistance

transistor a semiconductor electronic component that allows a small amount of charge to control the flow of current through it; transistors are useful for amplification or, in computer circuits, as on-off switches

voltage a measure of the force acting on charges; in an electric circuit, voltage causes a current to flow

FURTHER READING AND WEB SITES

BOOKS

Bloomfield, Louis A. *How Things Work: The Physics of Everyday Life,* 3rd ed. New York: Wiley, 2005. A college-level text that is easy to understand and covers a wide range of phenomena.

Bodanis, David. *Electric Universe: How Electricity Switched On the Modern World.* New York: Crown Publishers, 2005. A narrative of the history and development of electricity, highlighting the pioneers who helped establish the principles and applications.

Calle, Carlos I. *Superstrings and Other Things: A Guide to Physics.* Bristol, United Kingdom: Institute of Physics, 2001. Explains the laws and principles of physics, including electricity and magnetism, in a clear and accessible manner.

Campbell, Wallace H. *Earth Magnetism: A Guided Tour through Magnetic Fields.* New York: Academic Press, 2001. A thorough discussion of Earth's magnetic field and its many effects.

Coleman, Mark. *From the Victrola to MP3, 100 Years of Music, Machines, and Money.* Cambridge, Mass.: Da Capo Press, 2003. Music-making machines, from past to present.

Davis, L. J. *Fleet Fire: Thomas Edison and the Pioneers of the Electric Revolution.* New York: Arcade, 2003. A history of the development of the electrical industry.

Gibilisco, Stan. *Electronics Demystified.* New York: McGraw-Hill, 2005. A straightforward and accessible explanation of the fundamentals of electronics.

Kruszelnicki, Karl. *Fidgeting Fat, Exploding Meat and Gobbling Whirly Birds.* New York: Wiley, 1999. Scientific answers to a large number of puzzling and quite often humorous questions of nature and technology.

Lord, John. *Sizes.* New York: HarperPerennial, 1995. Puts into perspective the vast range of sizes and magnitudes of objects.

Sekuler, Robert, and Randolph Blake. *Star Trek on the Brain: Alien Minds, Human Minds.* New York: W. H. Freeman, 1998. Electricity is crucial to brain function. This book explores the brain and how it works, with many references to the characters and aliens of the television and movie series *Star Trek.*

Suplee, Curt. *The New Everyday Science Explained.* Washington, D.C.: National Geographic Society, 2004. Concise scientific answers to some of the most basic questions about people and nature. Richly illustrated.

Swartz, Clifford. *Back-of-the-Envelope Physics.* Baltimore: Johns Hopkins University Press, 2003. A collection of simple but intriguing calculations covering a variety of phenomena from large to small, showing the usefulness of physics and elementary mathematics in understanding the world.

White, Ron, and Timothy Edward Downs. *How Computers Work,* 8th ed. Indianapolis: Que, 2005. All about the computer, including the inner workings, with a wealth of illustrations.

WEB SITES

American Institute of Physics. "Physics Success Stories." Available online. URL: http://www.aip.org/success/. Accessed on April 14, 2006. Examples of how the study of physics has impacted society and technology.

American Physical Society. "Physics Central." Available online. URL: http://www.physicscentral.com/. Accessed on April 14, 2006. A collection of articles, illustrations, and photographs explaining physics and its applications, and introducing some of the physicists who are advancing the frontiers of physics.

California Energy Commission. "What Is Electricity?" Available online. URL: http://www.energyquest.ca.gov/story/chapter02. html. Accessed on April 14, 2006. Discusses the basics of electricity in easily accessible language.

Davidson, Michael W., and Florida State University. "Molecular Expressions: Electricity and Magnetism." Available online. URL: http://micro.magnet.fsu.edu/electromag/index.html. Accessed on April 14, 2006. Links to tutorials on capacitance, inductance, generators and motors, CDs, and other electrical and magnetic topics.

Eck, Joe. "Superconductors." Available online. URL: http://superconductors.org/. Accessed on April 14, 2006. Great Web site containing articles on the history, uses, and types of superconductors, and news and explanations of ongoing research.

Electricity Forum home page. Available online. URL: http://www.electricityforum.com/. Accessed on April 14, 2006. Contains information on the use and production of electricity, with sections devoted to static electricity, solar electricity, hydroelectricity, electricity generation, and many other topics.

Epilepsy.com. "Epilepsy and the Brain." Available online. URL: http://www.epilepsy.com/epilepsy/epilepsy_brain.html. Accessed on April 14, 2006. A series of articles on the electrical aspects of normal brain function, and what goes wrong in the set of disorders known as epilepsy.

Exploratorium: The Museum of Science, Art and Human Perception. Available online. URL: http://www.exploratorium.edu/. Accessed on April 14, 2006. An excellent Web resource containing much information on the scientific explanations of everyday things.

Global Hydrology and Climate Center (GHCC). "Lightning and Atmospheric Electricity at the GHCC." Available online. URL: http://thunder.msfc.nasa.gov/. Accessed on April 14, 2006. A Web site devoted to the activities of a group of scientists at the Global Hydrology and Climate Center who study lightning and atmospheric electricity. An essay on lightning's causes and effects is included.

HowStuffWorks, Inc., home page. Available online. URL: http://www.howstuffworks.com/. Accessed on April 14, 2006. Contains a large number of articles, generally written by knowledgeable authors, explaining the science behind everything from computers to electromagnetism.

Jenkins, John D. "Development of the Electromagnet." Available online. URL: http://www.sparkmuseum.com/MAGNET.HTM. Accessed on April 14, 2006. The history of electromagnets, including illustrations of some of the many devices that have been made with electromagnets over the years.

National Aeronautics and Space Administration (NASA) home page. Available online. URL: http://www.nasa.gov/. Accessed on April 14, 2006. News and information from the United States agency devoted to the exploration of space and the development of aerospace technologies. A Web site that contains a huge number of resources, including photographs, movies, and clear and accurate explanations of the science of space exploration.

Stern, David P. "Magnetism." Available online. URL: http://www-spof.gsfc.nasa.gov/Education/Imagnet.html. Accessed on April 14, 2006. Discusses the fundamentals of magnetism and provides links for further information.

University of New South Wales, School of Physics. "Electric Motors and Generators." Available online. URL: http://www.phys.unsw.edu.au/~jw/HSCmotors.html. Accessed on April 14, 2006. An excellent Web page that contains information on all types of electric motors, generators, and transformers, with plenty of animated illustrations.

INDEX

141